TO PAY OR NOT TO PAY?

TO PAY OR NOT TO PAY?

What happens if you don't pay the Poll Tax

Alan Murdie
and Len Lucas

GREEN PRINT

First published in 1990 by
Green Print
an imprint of the Merlin Press,
10 Malden Road, London NW5 3HR

© 1990 Alan Murdie and Len Lucas

All rights reserved. No part of this publication may be reproduced, stored in a retrieval system, or transmitted, in any form or by any means electronic, mechanical, photocopying, recording or otherwise, without the prior permission in writing of the publisher.

ISBN 1 85425 054 X

1 2 3 4 5 6 7 8 9 10 : : 99 98 97 96 95 94 93 92 91 90

Typeset from the authors' disks by Saxon Printing Ltd., Derby

Printed in England by Biddles Ltd., Guildford, Surrey on recycled paper

Contents

Introduction	1
Poll Tax – An Outline	2
The New System of Raising Money for Local Services	7
Community Charge or Poll Tax?	9
The Local Government Finance Act 1988	11
Protecting Yourself at Law	12
The Poll Tax Register	14
The Poll Tax Canvass	20
Paying the Poll Tax	22
Collective and Standard Community Charge	25
Joint and Several Liability	27
Exemptions	29
Community Charge Benefit	32
Unpaid Poll Tax	38
The Magistrates Court	41
Recovery of Poll Tax Debt	54
Attachment of Earnings	56
Deductions from Income Support	63
Distress	67
Imprisonment	78
Poll Tax Appeals	82
Cornish Tin Mines and the Stannary Parliament	85

Introduction

To many people the law is a mystery. This is even more so with the Poll Tax where confusion and fear exist even on the part of many who can afford to pay it. This guide attempts to answer some of these concerns, particularly as regards what will happen to those who do not or cannot pay their Poll Tax bills. In reality people have many more legal rights than they tend to assume.

We do not answer every question here – nor could we. Some areas of the law are unclear and, as with any new law, it is impossible to predict exactly how the courts will interpret many aspects of the legislation. What we have attempted to do is give clear and concise legal information to those who want it in a way that is understandable (we hope!) to non-lawyers.

This guide does not aim to persuade people to withhold their Poll Tax. That is a decision for individuals. Rather, we seek to explain the consequences of non-payment in simple terms for anyone as the law currently stands in England and Wales. We believe people have a right to know this information and that so far little effort has been made to explain it by the government, local authorities or lawyers.

We also give a brief introduction to the many issues surrounding the Poll Tax and a short explanation of the new system for funding local authority services.

'*To Pay Or Not To Pay?*' arose from our work for the Poll Tax Legal Group, a voluntary advisory and consultancy organisation founded by ourselves. It is an updated, revised and extended version of a pamphlet entitled '*"What will happen if I don't pay the Poll Tax?" Legal Questions and Answers on the Community*

Charge' first published in March 1990 before the first Poll Tax non-payment cases came before the courts in England and Wales. We include important information and lessons arising from those cases and detail new information which has come to light from our continuing research.

Warning: *The law changes rapidly and Poll Tax legislation has changed very rapidly indeed, particularly as the government has found the Poll Tax becoming an increasing political disaster in terms of being a vote loser. We therefore must state that the law and information contained in this guide is as believed accurate by us at the time of publication. This guide is undoubtedly not the last word on Poll Tax legislation and its legal implications – nor could it be.*

Poll Tax – An Outline

The introduction of the Poll Tax satisfies an election pledge made by the Conservative Party in their 1979 election campaign. Or rather the abolition of the rating system, necessary to its introduction, does. On coming to power in 1979, the Conservative government, although pledged to getting rid of the rates, had no planned alternative to put in its place.

A decade later and after considerable legislative measures extending central government control over local government expenditure an alternative has been found and put into operation. It is a measure, however, that has caused a great deal of anger and opposition, not least within the ranks of the Conservative Party itself. It had even been previously discarded due to the complexity of a system that wished to tax every individual, in employment or

POLL TAX – AN OUTLINE

not. In 1981 a Green Paper *'Alternatives to Domestic Rates'* failed to produce a viable alternative, despite three options proposed. A following White Paper said of a Community Charge:

> "The tax would be hard to enforce. If the electoral register were used...it could be seen as a tax on the right to vote. A new register would therefore be needed but this would make the tax expensive to run and complicated, particularly if it incorporated a rebate scheme." (*Community Charge/Poll Tax, The Facts*. Rating and Valuation Association and the Association of District Council Treasurers, 1987)

The Poll Tax, however, returned in the 1986 Green Paper *'Paying for Local Government'*. The Poll Tax was now seen in a different light; the government have claimed it is fairer than the rating system and that it would strengthen the accountability of local government.

The tax is said to be fair on the grounds that as everyone in an area benefits from services like refuse collection, street lighting and so on it is only right that everyone should contribute toward them. A common image used in comparing the Poll Tax with the old rating system is that of the elderly widow living next door to a family of perhaps four wage earners, with both households facing the same rates bill. Under the Poll Tax the widow will pay only a quarter of that paid by the family of four. However, the opportunity for all to move into a lower rated property is lost completely with the Poll Tax. People can only move into other boroughs with lower levels of Community Charge.

The argument that the Poll Tax improves local electoral accountability is based on the notion that electors will measure the success of their council in providing services on the level of the bill they receive. Voters can now compare their Poll Tax bill with that of their neighbouring council, they can also compare it with the government estimated figure, by law printed on all Poll Tax bills. This argument ignores discussion of need or quality of services; it is implicit in the argument that services provided as cheaply as possible are in the best interests of the voter.

It is equally possible, however, to say that the Poll Tax neither

POLL TAX – AN OUTLINE

improves fairness or accountability. That the Poll Tax is a flat rate charge has led to severe criticism. Indeed the notion that even the poorest members of society should pay for local services is not only seen as immoral by many, but also runs against the traditions of almost every tax law in English legal history. The principle of graduated taxation, that is taxation linked to ability to pay, has been present in tax laws going back to the Dark Ages and the Dane Geld. The only exceptions are the Poll Tax Acts of 1378 and 1380 (which helped prompt the 'Peasants Revolt') and a 'Hut Tax' imposed for some forty years in colonial Africa at the beginning of the century. No other country in the industrial world has a tax like it.

With regards to improving the accountability of local government it is argued that the Poll Tax takes a great deal of autonomy away from local authorities. This is lost to central government who have distributed grants according to a central assessment of local authority need since the Local Government, Planning and Land Act of 1980. Now, however, business rates are no longer under local control, and the government has further extended its influence over local government expenditure. In this respect, any increase in accountability would appear to be that of local government to Whitehall rather than that of local government to the local electorate.

A further argument against the Poll Tax is one of practicality. The desire to extend liability to almost every person over eighteen has left local authorities with an enormous task of keeping an up to date register of all adults in their area. This has also raised questions concerning privacy and civil liberties. In addition, as an individual form of taxation the number of defaulters is considerably higher than that of the old rating system. This will all add a great deal of pressure on to already over-stretched local authorities.

The Poll Tax itself is not without contradictions. The system of safety nets, aimed to ease the introduction of the charge, run counter to the philosophy that people should pay for what they get, as some areas subsidise others. Poll Tax capping also contra-

POLL TAX – AN OUTLINE

dicts the notion that a local authority should be judged by the ballot box on the basis of the charge it levies for the services it provides. A startling contradiction is the expense and complexity inherent in a system proposed by a government committed to cutting local authority expenditure and 'streamlining' services. The Poll Tax is an incredibly inefficient form of taxation. This could lead to the conclusion that the cost must appear to be worth the imagined benefits of such a radical change in local government.

In this respect it might be wrong to see the Poll Tax as an isolated item of legislation. Rather it should be seen as part of a programme of change in which the Poll Tax is an early stage.

At the extreme there is an envisaged society whereby local authority areas are run by managers and rather than vote, individuals choose the area in which they wish to live, by the services it provides and the charge it imposes for them. This has been termed the Tiebout hypothesis after a writer called Charles Tiebout. There are obvious flaws in this logic, not many people can just get up and move on the sole grounds of a high local tax, and indeed those least able to move will probably be in high tax areas. It also ignores the relationship of services to needs; those areas with most needs will need more services and by definition the people living there will be those least able to afford to pay for them.

Despite these flaws, however, the impact of the Poll Tax has striking similarities with this model of local government; the highest Poll Taxes are generally to be found in inner city areas, areas of highest deprivation. It is also a clear intention of the Poll Tax that people begin to value local services in purely monetary terms; terms such as quality or need no longer have relevance.

The implementation of the Poll Tax can also be seen as a method of indirectly achieving other political and ideological aims of the government. In order to run the Poll Tax local authorities have been forced to recruit private services of all kinds from computer firms to bailiffs. With computer programmes having to be re-written with every change in Poll Tax legislation, this feature alone means a continual drain on local authority resources into the private sector.

POLL TAX – AN OUTLINE

To keep Poll Tax bills low local authorities are forced to cut services again clearing the way for free market provision of services. Reducing bills has also meant the sell-off of property on a far greater scale than the Council house sales of the past decade. Large areas of open public space are now under threat including playing fields, sporting facilities and burial grounds. The nineteenth century position where parks, beaches and cemeteries were all in private hands may thus be re-emerging, yet another aspect of the pledge of the Prime Minister to re-introduce 'Victorian values' into society.

The impact of the Poll Tax raises serious doubt as to whether the system will ever overcome its inefficiencies, and indeed raises the question as to whether it was really meant to work anyway. Those agencies that have the task of running the tax are faced with a seemingly impossible task. For example, it remains to be seen how a few hundred court officials, in Scotland, are to deal with over 800,000 people who have not paid their 1989 bill. Indeed, if Poll Tax was seriously meant to be recovered through legal action, why was the task not given to the Inland Revenue which has many thousands of staff and greater powers at its disposal to pursue tax evasion? In the long run the Poll Tax appears to be about removing democratically elected local government as a feature of our society altogether.

The New System of Raising Money For Local Services

There are three parts to the income local authorities now receive. These are government grant, Revenue Support Grant; business rates, the Uniform Business Rate; and the Community Charge or Poll Tax. The basis of the income the authority receives is the Standard Spending Assessment.

The Standard Spending Assessment sets a government target for local authority spending. In theory the government grant should be such that all Poll Taxes throughout the country are the same. The government assesses the needs of local authorities and gives that grant sufficient to enable that authority to charge the government-estimated Poll Tax. In 1990 this was £278.

However, where the government underestimates the needs of local authorities they must raise more money through the Poll Tax (where this happens a need to raise 1% more than the government estimate means Poll Tax rises by 4% because it is only 25% of Council income – most money comes from central government grants). Further differences in local Poll Taxes arise due to policy decisions of local authorities; some Councils have engaged in creative accounting, selling assets and cutting services and the degree to which local authorities have used reserve funds to lower the first year's Poll Tax varies. Where this has occurred there may be substantial increases in Poll Tax for 1991–92. In some cases it has been suggested that the government has also given more than is needed for certain Councils.

THE NEW SYSTEM OF RAISING MONEY FOR LOCAL SERVICES

What is Revenue Support Grant? Revenue Support Grant is paid to local authorities from central government. The grant accounts for the bulk of a local authority's income. The grant is calculated on the basis of the government conducted Standard Spending Assessment. It brings local authority income up to the level of income the government believes an area requires to provide for local needs. A consequence of the grant is that any expenditure a local authority incurs above the level set by government, and provided for by grant, must come from the Community Charge.

What is Uniform Business Rate? Uniform Business Rate (UBR) is a rate levied on business which replaces the old business rates. Unlike the old rates, set by the local authority, UBR is set by central government. In 1990 this has been done through a rate evaluation and the setting of a national rate poundage. The rate payable is calculated by multiplying the ratable value by the poundage; from 1990 this is to be linked to inflation. Revaluations will take place at 5 yearly intervals. UBR is paid by businesses into a central pool; the money is then redistributed to local authorities on the basis of population in each area.

Businesses can request a change in their ratable value up to 1st October 1990. If the local authority and business cannot agree the matter can be taken up as an appeal with the Valuation and Community Charge Tribunal. Proposals to change the value and appeals are also possible if something occurs that might have consequences for the value of a property.

What is the Poll Tax? The Poll Tax (or Community Charge) replaces the rates. Poll Tax raises around 25% of a local authority's income. It is levied on almost everyone over the age of eighteen. There are three types of Poll Tax; Personal, Standard and Collective. Most people will pay the Personal Charge. Standard Poll Tax is paid on vacant residential property and holiday homes. The Collective Charge is paid by people in short stay hostels and similar accommodation.

Why if more people pay Poll Tax is it as high or higher than my rates? Although more people are liable to pay the Poll Tax than was the case for rates there have been other changes in the system. For example, local authorities are no longer free to raise money from businesses. The government also underestimated inflation, a method of cutting real spending, when carrying out the Standard Spending Assessments. In addition the Poll Tax is a very expensive form of taxation; this has in itself added to the costs faced by local authorities.

Community Charge or Poll Tax?

With the government calling the Poll Tax the Community Charge and most people calling the Community Charge the Poll Tax, there has been an amount of confusion, with some people believing that the government have not only introduced the Poll Tax, but a Community Charge as well. The term Poll Tax is itself confusing, in that it is often assumed to mean a tax on voting. This is not entirely correct.

Is the Poll Tax a charge? In spite of being called the 'Community Charge' the way it operates does not match the normal use of the term 'charge'. A charge is most appropriately a term for a market transaction in which goods or services are exchanged for a fee: for example, you pay to get into a swimming bath, you pay for a television licence and so on. If you do not want a particular service, you can lawfully avoid it merely by not consuming it and so not paying for it. You cannot avoid Poll Tax by opting out from using certain services – litter must be collected whether you wish to pay for it or not (and whether you drop it or not!). Similarly the police must be paid, trading standards upheld, graves dug and so on.

Is the Community Charge a Poll Tax? Poll Tax might be a better term for the Community Charge. With a tax you are required to pay a sum of money even if you do not agree with the way that the revenue might be spent. For example you cannot legally refuse to pay income tax because you disagree with the government's nuclear weapons policy.

In addition the term 'poll' signifies that the tax is a tax per head of population. As the Community Charge is paid by individuals and liability rests on being an individual person it is a head or poll tax. In the initial discussions on Poll Tax it was also suggested that there was a link to voting.

Which term is correct? Neither term is particularly precise. The best name in legal terms would be 'Poll Rate'. This is because the method of determining the amount payable in Community Charge is the same as that used for rates. In the *'History of Local Rates in England'* (1927) by Professor Cannan the distinction lies in the fact that with a tax the law requires everyone liable to pay, whatever is gathered represents the final yield. There is no fixed sum, the taxing authority aims to gather as much as it can. With a rate the authority begins with a fixed budget figure of the money to be raised, and this is divided between those liable to pay. This is how the Poll Tax works except that unlike the old rating system the ratable value of property is not a relevant factor in deciding how much people pay.

The Local Government Finance Act 1988

The Poll Tax was introduced, in England and Wales, by the Local Government Finance Act 1988 (LGFA). The Poll Tax was introduced a year earlier in Scotland due to the Abolition of Domestic Rates Etc (Scotland) Act.

The Act gives an outline of the new system for funding local government. It does not give much information about the actual workings of the Poll Tax. It does not set down how much you pay, how it will work, or what will happen if it is not paid.

The Act gives wide powers to the Minister – the Secretary of State for the Environment – to make up the laws to bring the tax into force.

How does the Minister make these laws? The Minister makes laws through publishing Regulations, which are released after they have passed before Parliament, although MPs may not have the time or knowledge to examine them properly, if at all.

The Regulations are published as sheets or brochures called 'Statutory Instruments' (SIs). They have a date of publication and a serial number. These Instruments can be bought through bookshops.

Under the Local Government Finance Act 1988 the Minister has powers to draw up regulations on almost every aspect of the Poll Tax. The Minister has the power, and has used it, to issue regulations on: administration, determining who should pay, eligibility for reductions, and enforcement among other matters.

In the past such 'skeleton' legislation, giving powers to a politician to draw up regulations, was considered suitable only for emergency or extraordinary situations, for example war or civil emergencies such as Northern Ireland. Traditionally taxation has been thought too important to be left to regulations. The risk with regulations is that Parliament does not look at them properly. This is especially important in that they tend to be written in obscure, complicated language which even lawyers have difficulty in understanding. In addition Statutory Instruments are not easy to obtain for people in many parts of the country and they are costly. Even discovering they exist can be a major difficulty.

Protecting Yourself at Law

The law and the legal system are complicated – even for lawyers. Poll Tax law is complicated and, because it is a new law, its implementation is proving particularly difficult. Errors and mistakes of all kinds have already occurred and will undoubtedly continue to do so, throughout the lifetime of the Poll Tax. (The first three ever attempts to take people to Court for non-payment in England collapsed because of legal and administrative failures by the local authorities concerned.)

In order to protect yourself, there are a number of steps you can and should take in any legal dealings of any nature with your local authority and not just for the Poll Tax.

First of all, do not assume that local authorities are "Big Brother" – all-powerful organisations which have powers to do what they like. Local authorities have to follow the law – if they do not they can be taken to Court.

At law, local authorities are considered as having "legal person-

PROTECTING YOURSELF AT LAW

ality". This means that they have rights at law just like a physical human individual. Thus, a local authority can make contracts, buy and sell property, make investments or take people or corporations to court just like a human individual could. Similarly, if a local authority, via its staff, commits a legal wrong, fails to carry out a statutory obligation or is negligent, it can be sued through the courts, just as court action can be taken against an individual. With the Poll Tax, most local authorities are likely only to have a handful of staff who know anything about Poll Tax law. This is one reason why the rate of errors is so high.

Before you can take any action against a local authority, or if you are to successfully protect yourself against any local authority mistake (and remember such a mistake could result in the authority taking you to court) you must have evidence which you can produce to support your case.

Listed below are some simple but very important precautions to ensure you have evidence and to protect you from the effects of any errors or mistakes which a local authority makes in implementing the Poll Tax.

1. Keep copies of anything your local authority sends you in writing.

2. Keep your own copies of anything you send to your local authority.

3. If negotiating with your local authority, never rely on any agreements or promises made to you over the telephone. Always get any agreements confirmed in writing – it is impossible to prove anything said over the telephone.

4. If you have a meeting with any local authority official or anyone else acting on their behalf try to have a friend or advisor with you who can act as a witness for what was said at any later stage, or get the agreement in writing. If a matter becomes legally contentious at a later stage it is important that you have some evidence to produce in order to prove your side of the story.

5. If an authority makes an error get in touch with them as soon as possible. Matters are more likely to get worse if an error is not picked up quickly and brought to their attention.

The Poll Tax Register

Before anyone can be billed for the Poll Tax the local authority has to know that the person exists. Indeed the Poll Tax requires all those liable to pay the tax to be on the Poll Tax register. Poll Tax legislation requires each local authority to draw up a list of everyone eligible to pay in their area. This register must be kept up to date. Local authorities have a financial incentive to ensure its accuracy – a small percentage of people unregistered will show up as an increase in the Poll Tax bill for the area. The Community Charge Registration Officer has wide powers to secure information on individuals who might be liable to Poll Tax. The register can also be back-dated for up to two years, in order to include those who may have been omitted when the list was first compiled.

The registration process will be repeated each year. In 1989 it was intended to be drawn up by local authorities sending forms to each household in their area asking for information. Many of these forms fell foul of the Data Protection Act, which restricts information that can be held on computer. The local authority can also use many other sources such as old rating lists or housing records. Information can also be gained from companies such as British Telecom or British Gas. Local authorities might also use door to door canvassing using either their own employees or an agency.

Who is sent a form? The registration form is sent either to 'The Occupier' of a household or a named person generally taken as the person who is 'head' of the household, or any person who is shown on other lists as living there. So you may receive a form addressed to the person or persons who received the old rates bill.

THE POLL TAX REGISTER

What is a 'responsible person'? A responsible person is the person that the form is sent to, or the person who fills the form in. The responsible person must ensure the form is filled in correctly. If the responsible person knowingly gives wrong information or the form is not returned, they may be liable to a penalty. In practice it is hard to prove whether a form was deliberately not returned, it could have been lost in the post, or a canvasser may have talked to a visitor rather than an occupier.

If the form has a name on it then that person has been designated as the responsible person. If it is addressed to the occupier the person filling it in becomes the responsible person. The responsible person can appeal against being designated as such and can also appeal against any penalty that may be imposed.

Who decides which information can be used to compile the register? Information used (e.g. rates, housing lists etc.) is at the discretion of the Community Charge Registration Officer. The CCRO has a large financial incentive to use all the information that is available. Non-registration of eligible persons means the Poll Tax bills rise. You may well be automatically registered.

Can I see my entry on the register? Yes, indeed you should be sent a copy to check for errors each time you register. If you wish to see your entry you should contact your local authority. The register is meant to be open at any reasonable place or time for inspection.

Can I see another person's entry? This depends on what the Community Charge Registration Officer says. The Local Government Finance Act 1988 neither permits nor forbids members of the public examining extracts of another person listed on the register. This is at the discretion of the Community Charge Registration Officer.

THE POLL TAX REGISTER

What if I am not on the register? The Community Charge Regulations (S.I. 438 1989 section 3) says that a person who has reason to believe s/he is, or has been, subject to a Community Charge after December 1st 1989 shall inform the registration officer accordingly.

On one interpretation this could mean that everyone should write to the Community Charge Registration Officer and tell them that they believe they could be subject to a Community Charge! But since this section in the regulations appears under the 'Duty to Supply Information to Registration Officers' and mentions December 1st 1989, it is suggested that it relates to unregistered people.

However, the ignorance of the duty to register would not amount to a defence, millions of people are undoubtedly unaware of this duty, but the Act does not impose any penalty.

When should I inform the Registration Officer that I feel I may be liable to Poll Tax? The regulations require that you tell the registration officer within 21 days. Legally, it seems as pointless as a law saying you should give yourself up to the police if you commit a crime. Unless the authority knows you exist (in which case they will send you a form) it cannot be complied with. If the authority does not know who you are or of your existence they cannot take action against you. No punishment is listed, although you can be liable for up to two years' back Poll Tax if you are subsequently registered and were living in the relevant area over those two years. Absurd though this Regulation is, it reflects how heavily the Poll Tax depends on the compliance of individuals in order to work.

What if the information on the register is wrong? If information on the register is wrong the law requires that you inform the registration officer. The law says that a person who is shown on the register and has reason to believe the item concerned is incorrect or incomplete or not up to date must inform the registration officer.

There are plenty of reasons why you may not be aware of inaccuracies. You are meant to be sent a copy of your register entry to check. However, if you do not receive such a copy you will not know unless you make an effort to check your entry. If you are moving you should ensure that your entry is removed.

Can the local authority ask for information in addition to that requested on the form? Yes, the local authority can write to you and request that information it deems necessary to carry out the functions of registration, or administering the Poll Tax. However, the wording of the Act suggests that if you are exempt from the tax and the registration officer is aware of this you need not supply information. Otherwise the regulations state that requested information must be supplied within 21 days of the request being made, if the information is in your possesion or control. If you have any doubts about the request write to your local authority and ask for clarification. REMEMBER: Keep all correspondence.

Can my name be removed from the register? Yes, if you believe you might be under threat of violence and the Community Charge Registration Officer agrees with you. The wording of the legislation states that the Community Charge Registration Officer has the power to exclude "any person". If you write to the registration officer, you might be asked to state why you believe you might be under such a threat. But, remember you need only be under threat, not actually experiencing violence. Indeed, from the wording of the legislation other people who might be omitted could include those who might help pinpoint the whereabouts of the person subject to the threat of violence. However, you will still be liable to the Poll Tax.

THE POLL TAX REGISTER

Is non-registration a criminal offence? Not in England and Wales. It is a civil penalty and those penalties are imposed at the discretion of the registration officer. Some authorities have chosen not to impose penalties either as a result of policy decisions or because they simply do not have the time or resources to pursue them. Others have imposed them or included them on the eventual Poll Tax bill. As it is a civil matter it is not an arrestable offence and the Police are not involved in anyway.

What penalties can a local authority impose? A local authority may impose a penalty on anyone who:

(1) fails without reasonable excuse to supply information on request from the Registration Officer
(2) knowingly gives information which is inaccurate.

These are civil penalties, not criminal ones. For a first refusal, or a knowing failure to supply accurate information, a penalty of up to £50 may be imposed. A second refusal or failure may result in a £200 penalty and this may be repeated for each subsequent failure. However, the local authority can only impose a further penalty where the person commits the same breach of duty.

What form will the penalty take? The penalty will take the form of either:

(a) an addition to your Poll Tax bill or
(b) a separate bill requiring that you pay the penalty within 14 days.

What if I do not pay a penalty? Penalties that are not paid may be added to the Poll Tax liability and ultimately recovered in the same way as unpaid Poll Tax. As a result, people who have not co-operated with registration and who do not pay, but have been entered on the Community Charge Register, will not be in a position much different from those who did register but do not pay their bill, except that their bills will have the penalty added on.

Where a 14 day notice is served, the penalty may be enforceable in itself, like an instalment of Poll Tax, and the Magistrates' Court could be used to recover the penalty alone, just as if it was unpaid Poll Tax. (See 'Magistrates' Courts'). Local authorities have differing policies on ths matter so there is no guarantee whether they will or will not try to collect penalties through the Courts.

As an example, in June 1990 the local authority in Poole, Dorset, took a 79 year old man to Court to recover £450 of penalties imposed upon him because of his repeated failure to fill in Poll Tax forms. Other local authorities (it is hoped) will not necessarily take such a severe approach. In such situations, penalties can only be considered punitive in nature. In order to impose a penalty and take a person to Court the local authority must know the identity of the person to begin with – in which case they could just enter their name on the register anyway.

Can I appeal against a penalty? Yes, you can appeal against the penalty. This right is given by section 23(2)(h) of the Act. It is very important that people use this right, otherwise the next stage in recovery could be the Magistrates' Court. If it reaches the Magistrates' Court it is too late to use any argument you could have used on appeal to the local authority – Poll Tax law does not allow the Courts to consider such arguments, no matter how valid they may be.

Where an appeal has been lodged, a local authority cannot impose a second penalty until the first appeal has been disposed of correctly. If an authority attempts to do so they will be acting unlawfully.

In some cases local authorities have dropped penalties merely because an appeal has been lodged as they simply do not have the time or resources to spend on appeals. Where a penalty is under appeal, it cannot be recovered through the Magistrates' Court. For procedure on appealing, see 'Appeals'.

Is my right to vote affected if I am not on the Poll Tax Register? No, failure to have your name on the Community Charge Register does not affect your right to vote – the Electoral Roll is a separate register. (Nor does failure to pay the Poll Tax threaten your right to vote). However, even the most inefficient local authorities are getting round to copying the Electoral Roll to make up for deficiencies in the Poll Tax Register. It is worth noting that in inner city areas, which have highly mobile populations, electoral roles are notoriously inaccurate and so may not make a good basis for the Poll Tax register.

The Poll Tax Canvass

Where Poll Tax registration forms have not been returned or where an authority is trying to get information that has not been included, they may send people round to your home to ask for the information. These are known as Poll Tax canvassers and may be employees of the local authority or workers of private companies hired by the Council to carry out the work. (In 1989 Chiltern District Council hired a cash collection firm which distributed teddy bears and badges to promote good relations. The same firm may be returning to peoples' homes as bailiffs.)

What powers do Poll Tax canvassers have? None, you do not have to answer any questions that canvassers ask. They have no power to force you to say anything, make you give any information in writing nor make you communicate with them in any way. You do not have to open your door to them.

Neither can they make you give them any information about

anybody else who might live in the house – for the simple reason you may not know the information, or you may be just a visitor or guest.

How does ignoring a canvasser affect my duty to supply information? The fact that you do not answer any enquiries from a Poll Tax canvasser does not take away your right to supply the information to the registration officer at a later date if you so wish, or to lodge an appeal.

Can I tell the canvasser to leave? Poll Tax canvassers should leave your premises when requested – and you should give them a reasonable time to leave. In theory, you could use "reasonable force" to remove a Poll Tax visitor who is a trespasser and does not leave within a reasonable time of being asked to leave. However, this can be risky.

What should I do if a canvasser calls? The first thing you should do is ask for identification. Do not open your door or let anyone in until you know who they are for sure.

Canvassers really should have some form of ID card with their photograph on it: check this. They should also have some form of verification, which might be a letter from the local authority; check that the names and other information on the card and letter correspond.

Certainly, if you are at all unsure of the canvasser's ID, do not let them in, or give them any information. If they are genuinely from the local authority they will understand your caution. If canvassers call and are not correctly identified it is a good idea to let your local authority know. Remember an incorrectly identified canvasser has arguably even less right to gain information than a correctly identified one.

Paying the Poll Tax

If you are on the Community Charge Register and do not come within an exempt category, you are required to pay either the Personal Community Charge, which most people will pay, or the Collective Community Charge to your local authority. If you pay a Standard Community Charge this will be in addition to a Personal or Collective Charge.

The bill which you receive for the first year's Poll Tax is payable from 1st April 1990. Poll Tax is payable from the 1st April in each subsequent year. You may pay the Poll Tax in ten instalments, which must be paid in consecutive months, or, you may be able to come to a private agreement with your local authority.

Who gets a bill? If you are an adult (over 18 years of age) you are liable to pay Poll Tax to the authority in which your "sole or main" residence is to be found, i.e. where you live most of the time, provided that you have been registered. (Unless you are in an exempt category – see 'Exemptions').

Can I get my Poll Tax paid for me? Rebates are available for people on low incomes, but the maximum rebate is only 80% of the full Poll Tax. If you are faced with a Poll Tax much higher than your current rates bill you may also qualify for transitional relief (see 'Community Charge Benefit').

PAYING THE POLL TAX

What is the Personal Community Charge? The Personal Community Charge is levied on every liable adult who is not subject to a Collective Community Charge. Each person receives their own bill and is personally responsible for paying it.

Can I or must I pay Poll Tax by instalments? You can either pay your Poll Tax in one go or pay in ten monthly instalments. If you wish to have a different arrangement this should be negotiated with the local authority before bills are issued. However, in practice, local authorities are more than likely to offer special arrangements to persons experiencing difficulties in paying.

What happens to my Poll Tax if I move? If you move out of the area covered by one local authority and into another you should apply to have your name removed from the old authority's register. If you do not, you can be held liable for the Poll Tax in that area for two years or until the error is corrected.

If you move you will become liable for Poll Tax in your new area from the day you have your sole or main residence there. The amount to be paid will be the daily rate that has been fixed by the charging authority multiplied by the number of days you have your sole or main residence there.

If a person moves into a particular local authority area and does not appear on the register and then moves from this area, the person cannot be held liable for any Poll Tax in any action brought by that local authority.

Can the local authority make me pay in a particular way? Local authorities are very keen to persuade Poll Tax payers to pay by direct debit, that is to grant your local authority the right to deduct Poll Tax from your bank account (if you have one). This is because it is more convenient for them and the banks. It has even been suggested, by way of TV commercials, that this form of payment can 'make it easy on yourself' – it may be realistic to expect it is their own financial security they are really concerned about. However, they cannot force you to pay by direct debit, or indeed through any particular method. Direct debit is of course impossible for an estimated 9 million people who do not have bank accounts. If you are already paying the Poll Tax by direct debit you are perfectly within your rights to cancel it.

REMEMBER: you can pay in any way you choose be it by cheque, postal order or cash; your local authority cannot force you to pay in any particular way.

Is it a good idea to sign a direct debit form?

No, in this case it is like signing a blank cheque to your local authority. Direct debits are not a good idea for expensive matters such as Poll Tax, given that clerical errors may occur. If an error is made you may have more money taken from your account than you expect.

In legal theory you could certainly recover the money as soon as the error is detected. But this could take a long time and may lead to difficulties in sorting the matter out. Local authorities have recognised the "current scepticism of some debtors concerning this method."

Collective and Standard Community Charge

When am I likely to pay Collective Community Charge?
You may pay Collective Poll Tax if you live in a house containing a number of bedsits, some hostels, bed and breakfast hotels and similar accommodation. The exact details are at the discretion of the Community Charge Registration Officer of the relevant local authority. Where a Collective Poll Tax is charged the landlord can keep 5% of the tax for administrative costs.

What is the purpose of Collective Poll Tax? Its purpose is to make operation of the Poll Tax simpler. Where there are a large number of residents who often move it would be even more impractical to have such residents registering at every change of address.

How is it assessed and paid? The landlord is asked by the local authority how many people normally live at the premises. The landlord is then charged the sum of those Poll Taxes, this is then passed on to the residents. You should pay the equivalent of 1/365th of that local authority's Personal Charge per day (1/366th in a leap year). You pay your landlord this sum monthly unless you make other arrangements with your landlord.

Can I claim rebates? Yes, you are still entitled to a rebate, which may be paid directly to you, in a voucher form, by the local authority. But, you will still have to pay at least 20%.

COLLECTIVE AND STANDARD COMMUNITY CHARGE

What if I am paying Personal Poll Tax but stay at a bedsit subject to Collective Poll Tax? If the bedsit is not your main home you may have to pay both the Collective and Personal Charge.

When am I liable to Standard Community Charge? You are liable for Standard Community Charge if you have a residential property which is not your sole or main place of residence. You cannot get a rebate for the Standard Charge.

Who determines if a residence is a sole or main residence? The Community Charge Registration Officer decides whether you are liable for Standard or Personal Charges at a particular residence. You can appeal (see 'Appeals').

Am I still liable if I am moving house? No, not for the first three months if you have vacated the property. After this period you will be liable for Standard Community Charge. If you go into residential care you will not be liable for Standard Poll Tax for at least 12 months.

How much will Standard Community Charge be? Local authorities set Standard Charges but they cannot be more than twice the Personal Charge, all such property must have the same Standard Charge.

Can I pay more than one Poll Tax? Yes. If you have more than one home you will pay Personal and Standard Poll Taxes. If you had a main residence, a holiday home and had to stay at a bedsit for some reason you could be paying all three charges.

Joint and Several Liability

If you are married, or living as if you were married, you are jointly and severally liable for the Poll Tax. This means you must pay any debts your spouse incurs. If your spouse is under 18 joint several liability does not arise.

This is an important aspect of the Poll Tax, and to some extent contradicts the aim of individual liability. It must be stressed that Poll Tax can be recovered from either partner, whether or not they incur the debt. One case that came to the notice of the authors was that of a woman, whose husband had died sometime before bills were issued. Whilst her husband had been sent a bill, she had not received one. In this situation if the husband's tax remained unpaid, as it was likely to, the woman would be taken as liable for it and could have faced Court proceedings to recover the debt. Such clerical errors undoubtedly cause a great deal of distress. But they should be brought to the attention of the local authority *as soon as is possible*.

What happens if I get married? If you get married during a Community Charge year (e.g. April 1990–91) only part of the Personal Community Charge bill will be jointly and severally liable – that part after the marriage.

The fraction of Community Charge for which joint and several liability arises is determined by the fraction:

$\frac{A}{B}$ = fraction of chargeable amount for J & S liability

where A = the number of days on which the couple were married to each other and the spouse is 18 or over within the

JOINT AND SEVERAL LIABILITY

chargeable period and B = the number of days in the chargeable period.

If you are getting married during the chargeable period, joint and several liability does not apply on the day of the marriage but only on the whole days afterwards. For those separating, the day the marriage is dissolved is not included in the fraction.

The concept of joint and several liability only applies to those married in the eyes of the law and does not apply to lesbian or gay couples, or family relationships – e.g. children of the household who are liable or other relatives living under the same roof.

What does 'living as if you are married' mean? There are a number of grounds which are used to decide if a couple is living as if married. They are the same as those used for social security and include: being of opposite sexes, sharing of finances, living in the same household, having a sexual relationship, having children, being known by friends/neighbours as a married couple, having a stable relationship. In practice, proving any of these could be very difficult for a local authority.

Exemptions

Before the question of what happens to those who are unable or who decline to pay the Poll Tax arises, the issue of exemptions must also be considered. Since the original intention that all voters should pay the same amount in Poll Tax was first expressed by the government, various exemptions have been granted – and more may yet be granted or extended.

Who is exempt? Those listed as exempt in the Local Government Finance Act 1988 and the Personal Community Charge (Exemptions) Order 1989 are:

- Persons resident in NHS hospitals.
- Persons in residential care, or hostels or homes providing a substantial level of care.
- The severely mentally impaired.
- Members of religious communities.
- Persons taken to hospital under the Mental Health Act 1983
- Persons staying in some short-stay hostels or night shelters.
- Homeless persons sleeping rough.
- Persons over 18 but still at school.
- Volunteers working on low pay for charities, such as Community Service Volunteers.
- Students studying in Northern Ireland or Scotland.
- American servicemen and other members of visiting forces.
- Government spies.
- Convicted prisoners and those on remand (except those detained for debt through Poll Tax or associated fines).

EXEMPTIONS

What does 'severely mentally impaired' mean? The Local Government Finance Act originally gave two definitions of what constituted being "severely mentally impaired". These two definitions have now been reduced to one and as a result, a person is classed as "severely mentally impaired if he has a severe impairment of intelligence and social functioning (however caused) which appears to be permanent." This definition then raises the question 'what is severe impairment of intelligence or social functioning?' The designation of a person as exempt, or otherwise, under this provision is open to appeal under section 23(2)(a) of the Act. (See 'Appeals').

What constitutes a religious community? To constitute a religious community as recognised by the Local Government Finance Act 1988 such a community must fulfil two of the following principal occupations: prayer, contemplation or the relief of suffering, or education. (The Secretary of State has powers to add to these occupations). To be recognised as a member of such a community an individual must have no personal income or capital, and must be dependant on the community for his/her needs. (This does not include pensions from previous employment). In practice this is one of the biggest 'loopholes' to be exploited for gaining exemptions. England and Wales may be about to witness a religious revival unparalleled in modern times (outside Iran) and the appearance of more religious communities at any time since the Middle Ages.

For example, philosophy students have successfully obtained the benefit of this exemption after the pooling of resources and arguing that their time was devoted to contemplation.

What constitutes a homeless person? A homeless person is someone whose sole or main place of residence does not consist of a building, caravan or residential boat. Such a person must also have no fixed abode 'throughout the day' in 'England, Wales or elsewhere'.

EXEMPTIONS

What if I live in a tent? Tents are not included among the classes of dwelling mentioned in the legal definition of homes. As a result, it appears to be the case that if your sole or main residence is a tent, which you move from site to site, you will be exempt from Personal Community Charge. Tepee villagers in Wales won an appeal on this point of law in spring 1990. However, if you have a house the exemption would probably not apply if you pitched a tent in the garden and at the very least there would be Standard Community charge to consider.

However, there appears to be no limit to the size of your tent to come within this exemption. Thus tents the size of circus 'big tops' or of the measure or luxury of those in the Arabian Nights could conceivably be exempt.

What if I am a student in Northern Ireland or Scotland? Students who attend courses and live in Scotland will pay the Scottish Community Charge. In Northern Ireland there is no Community Charge.

Can I appeal against being included on the register if I believe myself to be in an exempt category? Yes, section 23(2)(a) of the Act permits you to appeal against inclusion on the register as liable to the Poll Tax. If you have any doubts as to whether you should be exempt write to the Community Charge Registration Officer. (See 'Appeals'.)

Community Charge Benefit

Community Charge Benefit can be claimed by all those liable to the Personal or Collective Community Charge; if a person is liable for both then they can claim for both. Claiming, however, is not the same as receiving. Whether or not a claim succeeds depends on a wide range of factors. A local authority must assess each claim, taking income and needs into account. The assessment is carried out along prescribed lines. The most effective way to determine whether you may be entitled to Community Charge Benefit is to apply for it, but some pointers are given below. It is stressed, however, that if in doubt a person should claim, and even consider an appeal if circumstances warrant it. If a claim is successful a claimant will have the amount of benefit deducted from the Poll Tax bill.

In addition to Community Charge Benefit there is a 'Transitional Relief' scheme; although this was largely a measure to appease public opinion there are some important points to note.

What is Transitional Relief? Transitional Relief is a scheme to reduce any significant losses to previous rate-payers and their partners, and in a slightly different manner pensioners and people with disabilities, through the introduction of the Poll Tax.

For previous rate-payers the amount of relief is calculated on the basis of the government's estimated Poll Tax for an area. Previous rate-payers had any such relief, if relevant, deducted automatically from their Poll Tax bill.

However, *pensioners and disabled persons must apply to their local authority*. The cut off date for this is 1st October 1990.

COMMUNITY CHARGE BENEFIT

Pensioners and persons with disabilities should not be deceived by the fact they may already have had a bill showing a deduction for transitional relief. This may be because they were previous ratepayers. It may well be in the interests of any person in this situation to contact their local authority immediately and apply for further transitional relief.

Transitional Relief is a temporary measure and it is being phased out. In 1991–2 relief will be reduced by £13 and the same in 1992–3. Transitional Relief will be phased out altogether in 1993–4. If a person receiving relief moves, or their liability for Poll Tax ceases for some reason, then their entitlement ends. If a move is involuntary the person remains entitled provided they do not move outside of the local authority's area.

How does Transitional Relief affect my Community Charge Benefit?

Transitional Relief is deducted from the Poll Tax liability before Community Charge Benefit is assessed. It is possible, therefore, that receipt of relief might prevent the award of benefit, where the benefit received would be a small amount. If this results in a claimant being worse off the local authority should withhold relief and award benefit. If this occurs you should ensure you are granted Transitional Relief should your entitlement to benefit stop. Appeals against any decisions relating to Transitional Relief should be made to the local authority in the first instance. Write to the Community Charge section of the local authority. Continuing dissatisfaction can be taken up with the local authority's Housing Benefit/Community Charge Benefit Review Board; this is discussed below.

How do I make a claim for Community Charge Benefit?

Anyone can claim benefit at any time. Benefit can no longer be backdated to 1st April unless special circumstances arise. Each person liable to Poll Tax must make their own application; where couples are concerned (those defined as joint and severally liable, see above) only one application for both partners is necessary.

COMMUNITY CHARGE BENEFIT

Those receiving housing benefit before 1st April 1991 may have been automatically awarded Community Charge Benefit, if not they should have already been asked to complete a new form. People receiving income support should have received a form from the Departmnent of Social Security. Otherwise forms may have been sent out with Poll Tax bills. If you have not received a form then contact your local authority and ask for one. Remember, if you were eligible for benefit on 1st April 1990 and there is a good reason why you have not claimed benefit already you should point this out; it could result in benefit being backdated. If necessary appeal to the authority.

What might constitute a good reason for not applying for a rebate within the specified period for backdating?

A 'good reason' is a value term, it is, therefore open to some amount of interpretation. In this respect it may be partly subject to indivdual policy decisions of local authorities as they, rather than government, meet some degree of these costs. However, you might expect illness, misunderstaning of the claim form, receiving of incorrect advice or some similar situation to be a good reason.

How likely am I to get Community Charge Benefit?

Whether or not your claim succeeds depends on a large number of factors. The local authority assesses both your needs and your financial situation

The needs, translated into monetary figure, of an individual change depend on circumstances. For example, a person under 25 is said to need £28.80 per week, a person over 25 needs £36.70 per week, a couple with one or both partners over 18 needs £57.60 per week and a lone parent over 18 needs £36.70 per week. On top of these basic amounts are additions for dependants: a child under 11 means £12.35 per week is added to the parents needs, a child between 11 an 15 equals £18.25. These are termed dependant's allowances. Further additions to needs come from premiums awarded for special circumstances, for example, dis-

COMMUNITY CHARGE BENEFIT

ability, single parents, pensioners and so on. All of these factors are added up and assessed in relation to your income.

Your financial situation has two parts; income and capital. Capital can include: cash, savings, saving certificates and premium bonds, shares, property and lump sums from redundancy payments. If capital is greater than £16,000 there is no entitlement to benefit (in the case of couples this is the limit for joint capital); if capital exceeds £3,000 it is taken as generating an increasing income as it nears the £16,000 cut off point, so reducing your benefit entitlement. Some items of capital are not taken into account, for example, the home of an applicant, money put by for buying a home, compensation for loss of home possessions and personal possessions.

Income is taken as a regular payment over a set time span; thus payments made on a regular basis to elderly parents by grown up children may be taken as income if declared. Only income after tax (net) has been deducted is relevant. Wages, salaries, benefits, occupational pensions, maintenance payments and income from capital are all taken as income. Where special circumstances are encountered amounts of income are not taken into account to allow for them; these include single parents (£15, £25 from October 1990), couples (£10), single claimants (£5). In addition mobility allowances are not taken as income.

If you come within the limits on capital and your income is equal to, or less than, the assessment of your needs you qualify for maximum Community Charge Benefit, i.e. 80% of your Poll Tax. If, however, your income exceeds the assessment of your needs, then for every £1 that it exceeds your needs you lose 15p from the maximum benefit. That is until all entitlement ceases; the minimum claim possible is for 50p.

What would be a likely income in order to receive benefit?
As can be seen from the above, the calculations are complex and depend on individual circumstances. The range in which benefit might be awarded also varies with the level of Poll Tax in an area.

COMMUNITY CHARGE BENEFIT

If we were to take a typical Poll Tax of around £300, the upper limit on income resulting in benefit spans from a single person over 25 receiving £50 per week to an elderly couple receiving £125 per week. As Poll Tax rises so does the income level resulting in benefit. In broad terms you may be in with a chance of benefit if your net weekly income is £125 or less, but this does not mean you will get benefit, nor does it mean you will definitely not get benefit it your net weekly income exceeds £125. If in doubt claim!

What happens with a claim by a couple? Couples are assessed jointly for Community Charge Benefit, and they receive joint benefit. Couples, therefore, need only make one claim.

If one partner of the couple is a full time student, exempt, or under eighteen the partner liable to the full amount receives the full benefit, if benefit is awarded.

Can students claim Community Charge Benefit? Full time students are only liable for 20% of the Poll Tax. This is granted automatically. No claim is necessary. Students are not, therefore, eligible for Community Charge Benefit.

What happens if my circumstances change? If your circumstances change you have a duty to inform the local authority. Claimants must renew their claim after sixty weeks; you might be asked to do this at the end of the financial year.

Am I entitled to a rebate because I am on a pension? Not necessarily. Benefit is given on account of your income, as described above. If you have a low income you may succeed in claiming a rebate. If, therefore, your pension results in your receiving a low income you may succeed in claiming a rebate.

COMMUNITY CHARGE BENEFIT

I want to apply for housing benefit, but have not registered for the Poll Tax. Does this matter? Housing benefit and Community Charge Benefit use similar systems and the same forms. If you apply for housing benefit and have not registered for the Poll Tax, you could be automatically registered by your authority, or asked to register for Poll Tax. This is largely a policy decision to be made by your local authority.

What happens if I receive too much rebate? If the local authority gives you too much rebate you have to pay it back, unless the overpayment was a mistake of the local authority or Department of Social Security which you were unlikely to recognise at the time of overpayment. The authority can make you pay any excess payment back by adding the overpayment to your Poll Tax, making you repay it or by deducting the sum from other income-related benefits which you receive, with which the authority is connected. (LGFA 1988 Schedule 10).

How do I appeal against decisions regarding Community Charge Benefit? If you wish to dispute an issue relating to benefit first ask for a determination. This is a written statement detailing the decision on your benefit and enables you to challenge specific points. If you take the issue further you have six weeks in which to ask for a review. If you are still not satisfied the next step is to appeal to the Housing Benefit/Community Charge Benefit Review Board, a local authority board on which local Councillors sit, and in this respect it may be reasonably open to sympathetic decision making.

It may be possible, in certain circumstances, to have benefit increased above the limits set down by the system, although benefit will never exceed 80% of the Poll Tax. The extent to which this occurs is down to the local authority who have to fund any such increases.

Will I be taken to Court for not paying the Poll Tax if I am disputing my benefit claim? Disputing a benefit claim does not mean a Court cannot grant a liability order, to allow the authority to recover unpaid Poll Tax, against you. However a Department of the Environment practice note (number 15) says: "While it is not a defence against the issue of a liability order that a chargepayer is disputing the amount of entitlement to Community Charge Benefit... a Court is unlikely to award such an order while a determination is being formally reviewed."

Unpaid Poll Tax

Non-payment of the Poll Tax is not 'breaking the law' in the criminal sense. It is not a criminal offence to fail to pay the Poll Tax. It is a civil matter. If Poll Tax is unpaid, the person becomes liable in debt to their local authority. As with the old rating system the law states that there are a variety of steps by which a local authority can seek to recover the unpaid Poll Tax using the Courts. It is up to the local authority to pursue the matter – no-one else can begin legal action.

Local authorities have already accepted that a percentage of people will simply be unable to pay and they are resigned to the fact that it will simply be uneconomical to try and recover money from some debtors.

Can I be arrested for not paying the Poll Tax? No, non-payment is not an arrestable offence. An arrestable offence is normally one where there is a possible punishment of over 5 years imprisonment, where a police officer believes that an address given by a person could be false and a summons may prove ineffective, or where a statute creates a power of arrest. None of these grounds apply to Poll Tax non-payment by itself.

As non-payment is a civil matter, not a criminal one, the police are not involved. The only possibility of an arrest would arise at the very last stages of enforcement when other methods of enforcement have been exhausted and within restricted legal circumstances. Even then it will be at the discretion of the Magistrates' Court to order such an arrest.

An arrest could be made to get you to attend the court in the final stage where a court may order the imprisonment of a debtor, and where all other steps had failed. Such an arrest may involve bailiffs not police and is only possible where the Magistrates order it (see 'Distress' and 'Imprisonment').

What will an authority do if I don't pay? It is up to the local authority whether they take steps to try and recover money from people who do not pay the Poll Tax. It is at their discretion. The law says that they "may" take steps to get the money. Whether they will or not is another matter. Just as some local authorities have not imposed penalties on people who have refused to give information, whilst in theory they do not have power to wipe off Poll Tax debts, in practice there is no guarantee that they will pursue anyone who does not pay the Poll Tax for whatever reason, or that they even have the time, money or inclination to do so. For example, where a person cannot be traced the local authority has no alternative but to drop the matter.

What happens if a Poll Tax bill remains unpaid? A local authority cannot demand any payment of Poll Tax until a liable person is issued a bill. Where a bill remains unpaid, the first thing an authority must do is to send a reminder notice if they intend to pursue the matter. They are required by law to do this (Sections 20 and 28 of Statutory Instrument No 438 1989).

A local authority may serve such a notice any time after the instalment has been missed. Given the delays likely this could be

UNPAID POLL TAX

some considerable time. The local authority may want to know of your circumstances. They may send you other letters, but by law they have to send you at least one further notice. Where a particular instalment is unpaid, the local authority again has to serve a reminder.

What happens if I ignore this notice? Having received such a notice, you have 7 days from the date the notice was served, *not* from the date you first came to know about it, to pay. Where the amount remains unpaid, either wholly or partly, the person loses the right to pay by instalments and becomes liable for the whole year's remaining Poll Tax instalments in one lump sum.

When this happens a person still has seven days to pay off the remaining instalments for the year before the local authority obtains the right to use the Courts. If the money is not paid the local authority is then able to apply to the Court – a total of 14 days after the reminder notice was first sent. Accordingly, the local authority has no legal rights to recover any Poll Tax until two weeks after the reminder notice is sent. This is the minimum timescale available to the local authority after which it "may" apply to court for an order called a "liability order" against the person who is liable to pay Poll Tax. Again, it is up to the local authority if they take the necessary steps. This will be influenced in part by the level of Poll Tax default.

How does a local authority start legal proceedings? To start an action for the recovery of unpaid Poll Tax, a local authority applies to a Justice of the Peace or a Justices' Clerk to issue a summons. A day has probably been set in advance for Poll Tax hearings at the local Magistrates' Court and summonses are sent out to as many people as the local authority thinks it can deal with on one day.

When are summonses deemed served? The important date regarding these documents is the date of service. The specifications for service are outlined in legislation other than the Local Government Finance Act 1988. Service occurs when the document is:

- Delivered to the person concerned.
- Left at a person's last known address.
- Posted to a person's last known address.
- Posted to an address given as an address where such documents will be accepted.

As can be seen it is not necessary for a person to actually receive the summons for it to be correctly served. However, when a summons is served by post, service is deemed to take place at the time of delivery in the normal course of the post. In law second class post is deemed to take 4 days to be delivered and first class post 2 days, so a summons posted second class is deemed served 4 days after the date of posting, and a summons posted first class is deemed served 2 days after posting. (Interpretation Act 1978 s7, Local Government Act 1972 s233, General Rate Act 1967 s109).

The Magistrates' Court

The recovery of debt is usually carried out by civil courts called County Courts or through the High Court where sums of over £5000 are involved. However, the Government decided not to use the County Courts or High Court for the recovery of unpaid Poll Tax. Instead they chose the Magistrates' Courts which dealt with cases involving unpaid rates under the old rates legislation. The Magistrates' Courts were felt to be relatively quicker and more

THE MAGISTRATES' COURT

effective at recovering money. Magistrates' Courts try 97% of all criminal cases and deal with committal proceedings (the process of deciding which criminal cases should be sent to the Crown Courts). However, whilst dealing largely with criminal offences – everything from traffic offences to vandalism – the Magistrates' Courts also have a limited power in a number of civil matters including hearing licensing applications and dealing with child custody and care orders. The enforcement of Poll Tax comes within their civil role, as did the recovery of unpaid rates.

Nearly all of the 27,000 Magistrates ('Justices of the Peace') are lay people selected by local committees appointed under powers from the Lord Chancellor. Most do not have professional legal qualifications. They are intended to be representative of the local community and to some extent are drawn from supporters of the major political parties. However, as Magistrates are unpaid they tend to come from the wealthier sectors of society and those who have time to spare. There are few Magistrates from manual trades or employment as a result. There are also few Magistrates from ethnic minorities. However, it should not be assumed that Magistrates have no regard for the plight of Poll Tax debtors. At least one Magistrate has resigned from her post and others have expressed reservations about sitting at Poll Tax hearings. At the very least they will be conscious of the need to be seen to act as fairly as possible in the hearing of Poll Tax cases given the controversy surrounding the tax. Magistrates' Courts are usually held at some 565 locations in England and Wales. The 'Court' is not the building, but the Magistrates themselves, sitting together to hear the case. In theory a Magistrates' Court can be convened anywhere (except public houses or other licensed premises) although then their powers are more limited.

There is also a body of professional or 'Stipendiary' Magistrates who are lawyers of at least seven years standing who sit alone to try cases. However, it is not expected that they will play any significant role in Poll Tax enforcement.

The first step in recovering unpaid Poll Tax through the Magistrates' Court of Debt Recovery is to secure a liability order, allowing the local authority to proceed to recover their debt. This involves a Court hearing at which you can be present. The summons is the way used to ensure the debtor knows of a Court hearing. All these proceedings can be intimidating for the person involved and this is made worse by rituals of Court. Below we hope to provide an introduction to Magistrates' Court procedures, some background to the Court and an outline of what you can expect if you find yourself in the position of facing a Magistrates' Court.

The best way of getting an idea of what a Magistrates' Court is like is to visit one. With the exception of juvenile cases and some special cases, Magistrates' Courts are public and seating is available.

What will the summons say? A summons is a notice telling you to attend before the Court to explain why you have not paid. It will detail the place, date and time of your hearing and the sums concerned.

Can a mistake on the summons get me off? Quite often there will be a mistake on a summons – your name or street may be mis-spelt, for example. Many people imagine that such a mistake on the summons will get them off. This is probably a result of garbled ideas distilled from too many American TV legal dramas and media reports of cases which involved a technicality which was material to the case.

In reality, it is highly unlikely that any mistakes or errors on a summons can affect its validity. The summons merely tells you to come before the Court; it has no bearing on the facts of the case. The Court officials are, in any case, empowered to correct any defect on the summons. Only if the summons has not been signed or if the person is unidentifiable could there be grounds for challenge.

THE MAGISTRATES' COURT

Is there any time limit on a local authority making an application for a liability order to recover Poll Tax debt? Yes, a local authority must make an application within two years of the date on which the tax becomes due. So that a person who avoids registration until 1993 may be forced to pay Poll Tax from 1991, but could not be forced to pay any Poll Tax for 1990.

Do I have to attend the hearing? No. But it is in your interests to do so. Normally, if you do not respond to a Magistrates' Court summons you are in danger of being arrested, in order to bring you before the court. With the Poll Tax, the power of arrest has been specifically taken away, presumably in the hope that people will not attend. This is because proving cases against large numbers of people takes up too much in the way of time and resources.

Under the old rating system, few debtors ever attended Court and orders were drawn up against them in their absence, with the Magistrate merely signing a list of names of all those the local authority alleged had failed to pay. Both local authorities and the government are undoubtedly hoping that the same situation will arise with the Poll Tax. Do not be surprised if local authorities use your local press or radio to put out statements to discourage debtors from attending. You should not be put off by such statements.

What happens if I do not attend? If a person does not attend a hearing when summonsed, the local authority will be able to obtain a liability order very quickly indeed, which could mean they will use any of the methods for recovering Poll Tax immediately.

If you do not attend a hearing it will mean that you will be denied the opportunity to raise any defences you may have against a liability order. Nor will you be able to raise any other matter which might merit an adjournment or further consideration by the Court. As the Poll Tax is a tax on every individual, there may well be individual circumstances particular to your own case which have legal significance. Any such arguments deserve a hearing in Court. It is for the Court to decide who has the legal rights.

Failure to attend will also mean that the local authority will not be put to the test of proving its case in full and any errors in Court procedure or evidence which would otherwise stop the granting of a liability order may well go unnoticed where the hearing is uncontested.

It should never be assumed that just because someone threatens to or actually does take a person to Court they can or will actually succeed in proving their case on the day. Local authorities lose civil cases all the time. With the Poll Tax there is also the added problem that a new and unfamiliar piece of legislation is involved and much of the law is uncertain as yet. There is the ever present danger of a local authority error because the numbers of people involved are so large. These are all further reasons why debtors should attend and why anyone with an arguable case should come to court and raise it in full.

Can I get my case adjourned to another day? If you are unable to attend Court through illness or if you have a good reason as to why you cannot attend on the day mentioned on the summons, you can usually arrange to get a case adjourned to another day, probably several weeks in the future – if not longer.

You should telephone the Clerk to the Justices at the Magistrates' Court concerned, as soon as possible after receiving the summons, and ask for your hearing to be adjourned for at least two weeks.

In theory, you could arrange an adjournment on the morning of the hearing itself, provided you contact the Court before the time mentioned, but the Clerk may not agree to such a late application. Accordingly, it is much better if you arrange the adjournment well in advance.

In practice, Clerks are usually only too willing to arrange an adjournment with notice, as it reduces the work-load on the particular Court day. Much time is already taken up in the Magistrates Court system just adjourning cases to another day because of the existing shortages of Court time and qualified Court staff. The Poll Tax is only going to worsen the situation.

THE MAGISTRATES' COURT

What should I do on the day of the hearing? Court summonses are likely to specify a time from 10 o' clock in the morning onwards and hearings are likely to be set at half hourly intervals. However, do not be misled into thinking that the time specified on the summons will actually be the time your hearing takes place – it is merely an indication of what time the hearing was planned for. You should turn up on time for your hearing but be prepared for a long wait, possibly for hours. Cases almost always take longer than expected and long delays are just one of the extra hidden pressures, so it is best to expect them.

You are expected to wait at the Court and be in earshot when your name is read out. When you hear your name read out you should enter the Court room; ushers will show you the way. (If you are disabled it is probably best to notify the Court beforehand in order that they make any necessary arrangements).

You are unlikely to be on your own as the Court will probably deal with non-payment cases in "block bookings". That is, ten or twelve names will be read out together and you will enter the Court and appear before the bench in a group.

What happens if I go to court? Naturally enough, many people find the Magistrates' Court intimidating. Little if any guidance is given to a person as to what exactly is going on. However, the Magistrates are not in wigs and gowns, although they normally sit at a raised bench. Everyone is expected to stand when they enter or leave the Court. Quite often the officials make it intimidating.

As well as the Magistrates there will be a Clerk present in the Court. The Clerk is often the only legally qualified person present and will be either a solicitor or barrister. However, in the early stages of Poll Tax enforcement at least, the local authority will probably have its own lawyer to present its case. The Clerk advises the Magistrates on points of law and procedure. The Clerk will also put questions to each person summonsed.

The Clerk will ask each person their name, set out what the case is about and ask if you understand what the matter is about. After the preliminary questions are over, the Clerk may ask further questions of you at various stages. It is best to address the Magistrates directly, even though it is the Clerk who asks the questions. If you do not the Clerk may interrupt you and tell you to address the Magistrate. This will only add to the intimidating atmosphere.

You address the Magistrates as "Your Worships". Be polite at all times but do not be afraid to ask questions if you do not understand something. This is quite acceptable as neither the clerk or Magistrates are likely to know much about the Poll Tax as it is a new and complex piece of legislation.

Can I have a lawyer to represent me? You can have a barrister or solicitor to represent you, providing you can pay for one yourself, and that could cost as much if not more than your Poll Tax bill. Legal aid of any form is unlikely and in any case you will almost certainly have to pay a contribution.

If you are legally represented you need not attend personally but any liability order granted will take effect on you nonetheless.

Can anyone else help me in Court? A procedure that may be of use to an unrepresented debtor, and almost all debtors will be unrepresented, is the "McKenzie friend" procedure.

This allows a person who may be a professional lawyer acting free of charge, or anyone else to help a person in presenting the case of the debtor to the Court. The right to have a person as your McKenzie friend arises from the case of *McKenzie v McKenzie* in 1970 and is at the discretion of the Magistrates. However, in practice the right to a McKenzie friend is hardly ever refused.

If you wish to appoint somebody as your McKenzie friend, the person should enter the Court room with you when your name is called out and wait with you whilst the names of people summonsed are being checked. At some point the Clerk is likely to spot that there is an extra person appearing before them and ask who it is. At this point all the McKenzie friend should have to say is "I am here in connection with a McKenzie friend application," or something similar. No further questions are likely to be asked at

THE MAGISTRATES' COURT

this stage.

Once the local authority lawyer or employee has presented the local authority's case to the Magistrates, the Clerk will ask if anyone present has anything to say on the claims that you have not paid the Poll Tax. At this point the debtor should say: "Yes – and I would like to apply for Mr/Ms (give the person's name) to be my McKenzie friend". There appears to be nothing to stop a number of people summonsed applying to have the same McKenzie friend to help them.

What can the McKenzie friend do?

The McKenzie friend can take notes, quietly help and advise you and suggest questions to you to ask either the local authority witnesses or the Court. In certain cases, a Magistrates' Court may also allow the McKenzie friend to address the court if an argument in law arises and they think it in the interests of justice to hear him or her.

The Magistrates may also be prepared to read out a written statement of your case, prepared in advance, although questions may be asked instead. If you are going to read out a statement, have at least three copies available for the court as the Magistrates may adjourn to read it more closely.

What does the local authority have to prove?

Once the preliminary questions are over with the debtors assembled before the Magistrates, the local authority will present its case and their lawyer or employee will address the Magistrates. In early hearings the local authority may begin with a long discourse on various provisions of the Poll Tax legislation but this is not always the case. However, the local authority has to prove all of the following:

1. It has fixed a Community Charge.
2. That the debtor is on the register.
3. In the place of a debtor who is alleged to be jointly or severally liable with another person, that the local authority believes he or she is in a relationship with the person on the register.
4. That the Community Charge has been correctly demanded

(i.e. the bill is correct).
5. That the Charge has not been paid by the due date (that is at least 14 days after the date of the issue of the bill).
6. That the reminder notice has been sent.
7. That the sum due has not been paid within 7 days.
8. At least 7 days after the unpaid balance of the estimated amount has become payable, or the service of a notice (in the case of Collective Poll Tax) or the service of a reminder notice on the debtor, a SUMMONS HAS BEEN SERVED.
9. The full amount (including local authority costs) remains unpaid.

If the local authority can prove all the above points a liability order can be made by the Court. Before this is done you will be asked if you have anything to say. This will be your opportunity to speak, and if appropriate, give or call evidence on your behalf.

What defence may I have against a liability order being drawn up?

Poll Tax legislation was written with the same intention which underlies most road traffic offences; there are not meant to be any defences.

The law has been so tightly worded that the fact you may be an exempt category does not provide a defence in the Magistrates Court. The law says that any such arguments or disputes should be sorted out in an appeal to your local authority against registration – it is not a matter for the Magistrates and thus cannot stop a liability order being drawn up against you. Quite simply, if your name is on the register you are meant to be liable, whether it should be there or not.

However, despite these restrictions, there are, nonetheless, a number of defences against a liability order being imposed by a Magistrates' Court which may be of assistance in some cases. These may include:

You have actually paid the poll tax. It is unfortunately entirely possible that some people will receive summonses as a result of clerical and bureaucratic errors. If you have paid the Poll Tax you

THE MAGISTRATES' COURT

will have to prove it through evidence or get the matter adjourned so that the Council can do their own checks. This situation occurred when the first summonses were issued on the Isle of Wight in June 1990, the first local authority to attempt to recover Poll Tax in England.

There is no relevant entry on the Community Charge Register. If you are not on the Community Charge Register of a local authority at the time of the hearing, no liability order can be made.

In court you will be asked if you wish to challenge your register entry. You should exercise this right as it can never be assumed that the local authority have prepared their case correctly. If this is not mentioned you may raise it yourself, although it may take some minutes to check. If no entry can be found the case against you should be dismissed.

The local authority has not followed the rules in billing you or sending you a reminder. The local authority is expected to follow the statutory rules on obtaining the money and the reminder they send must be correct. This is a complicated area, not least because of the complex wording of the law as to what is involved.

Failure to keep within the regulations as to service led to the collapse of the first Poll Tax cases brought in England where the rules as to service were not followed. Insufficient time was allowed between the issue of a reminder notices and the service of the summons. Where second class postage is used, letters and summonses are deemed served four days after they are put in the post; in the case of first class post it is 2 days. A summons should be served 14 days before a hearing.

The person is on the register of two authorities. If your name is on two or more Poll Tax registers of different authorities for Personal Community Charge and one or more of the entries is subject to an appeal, you cannot have a liability order drawn up against you. You can only be liable for one Personal Community Charge at a time and that is wherever your sole or main residence may be.

Where the order is in relation to joint or several liability for another person's Poll Tax. You have a defence if you do not have the relationship alleged with the person who has incurred the debt, i.e. you are not married to them or you are not living with them as if married.

Are there any other matters to raise before the Court?

If your local authority has not worked out your community charge benefit or you are challenging the amount that you have been awarded, you should raise this before the Magistrates.

Whilst an outstanding dispute as to benefit entitlement does not amount to a defence, it is certainly good grounds to request an adjournment, in order that the dispute can be cleared up. Therefore, if your benefit has yet to be worked out or if it is subject to a determination, review or appeal (see section on benefits) you should raise this before the Magistrates and ask for your case to be adjourned until the local authority has been reached. There is a good chance that the Magistrates will grant an adjournment in such circumstances.

There may well also be individual grounds or matters relevant to a particular individual which could merit an adjournment in order that they may be looked into. Perhaps some private agreement with your local authority you have entered into or some indication you have had from them that you owe a different sum of money to that which they are claiming. Such grounds are impossible to predict until they occur, for they will vary in each individual case.

There may be other potential loopholes or technicalities lurking in the legislation which could be worth arguing if you are taken to court. Real life is always far more complicated than any lawyer or drafter of Parliamentary legislation can imagine; situations will always occur in practice that no-one ever expected and these may have a bearing. If in doubt raise it.

THE MAGISTRATES' COURT

Do I have to swear an oath? If you raise an issue that has a bearing on whether the local authority is entitled to a liability order against you, you may well be required to give sworn evidence on the matters concerned.

This means you have to swear an oath or promise to tell the truth and the procedure can take a number of different forms, depending on your beliefs. Christians are required to hold the New Testament and Jews to hold a copy of the Old Testament. Muslims are sworn on the Koran and Sikhs may be sworn on the Granth. Alternatively, if a witness has an objection to the sworn oath of a religious type they may give an "affirmation" to tell the truth.

What if I simply cannot afford to pay? Simple inability to pay the Poll Tax is not a defence in the granting of liability orders. The Magistrates' Court cannot deny a local authority the right to try and recover the unpaid Poll Tax at this stage of the proceedings. Only after the local authority have failed to recover the debt can the Magistrates rule on whether a debt should be written off. If a person simply cannot pay it may well be that the debt is written off in the end.

Can I make a speech to the Court? If you attempt to make a general speech to the court about your political or moral objections to the Poll Tax, the Magistrates are under no obligation to listen to you as the rights and wrongs of the Poll Tax will have no bearing on the facts of your case. Such comments are deemed political and do not have any legal significance. Magistrates' Courts are not forums for political debate or argument and you are likely to be told very quickly to desist from making such comments.

What are the costs likely to be? The local authority can add costs of obtaining the liability order from the court to the amount of outstanding poll tax claimed. Where a debtor does not attend costs will be nominal, spread among all those against whom the order is granted. Where a hearing occurs, legal costs will not be exorbitant – figures of £20 to £25 are around the level to be currently expected.

In any case, the local authority can only claim for those costs "reasonably incurred" which precludes expensive legal advice or representation in most cases likely to arise – not that most local authorities are in a financial position to commence expensive legal actions. The wording of the law suggests that local authority costs could be challenged if they are exorbitant.

What happens if a liability order is granted?

If after considering the evidence put before them the Magistrates conclude that the local authority has proved its case, and that you have no defence or any grounds for an adjournment, it must grant a liability order against you immediately.

However, whilst the granting of a liability order may seem very serious and a daunting event to the debtor, its significance should not be over-emphasised.

In cases of civil debt, all the Court does is decide and declare the respective rights of the parties involved. It does not help get the money – assuming the debtor has it available in any case. With the Poll Tax the local authority is faced with the task of trying to recover the money. The granting of a liability order does not mean that it will be able to do this.

Recovery of Poll Tax debts

There are a number of methods of debt recovery available to a local authority where a liability order has been granted.

What can the local authority do to recover debt? There are five ways that the authority can try and get the money from the debtor but only three are likely to be relevant to most debtors. These are an attachment of earnings order to deduct money from the wages or salary of the debtor, deductions from income support if the debtor is receiving it, or the seizure and sale of certain goods belonging to the debtor to pay off the debt, a process known as "distress" using bailiffs.

Which method a local authority selects will be a matter for it to decide. Its decisions will be influenced by the circumstances of the debtor concerned and the likely effectiveness of a particular method against that debtor. Other policy decisions may also come into play. If the debtor is in regular employment, an attachment of earnings order would be the most appropriate as it is the most likely way to secure the recovery of at least some of the money. For self-employed people or those on benefits other than income support, distress may be contemplated. However, because distress is an emotive way of obtaining payment some authorities may be reluctant to send in the bailiffs. Each of these methods has its own particular difficulties which may affect a local authority decision.

What other methods are there? Two other methods of recovery exist but they are highly unlikely ever to affect all but a small number of debtors liable for Community Charge.

RECOVERY OF POLL TAX DEBTS

In theory, where Poll Tax debts exceed £750, an authority could seek to use insolvency proceedings against an individual who would be declared bankrupt and the sum treated as a debt for the purposes of the Insolvency Act 1986. In practice this is unlikely to be of any assistance to a local authority pursuing an individual for Personal Community Charge and is therefore unlikely to be encountered.

Where Poll Tax debts exceed £1000 and involve Collective Community Charge a local authority can apply to the County Court for a charging order, giving the local authority a legal claim on the property of the landlord.

When can a local authority apply these measures? Once the local authority has obtained the liability order from the Magistrates' Court it can seek to recover the debt by one of the above methods, but a debtor can still pay off the debts before the measures take affect. In practice, there is likely to be some delay between the granting of a liability order and any enforcement. The speed of the authority will also be related to the level of non-payment in a particular area.

Can a local authority use more than one of these measures of collecting Personal Poll Tax at the same time? No, attachment of earnings, income support deductions and distress cannot be used together. The authority must stop proceeding with one method before it uses another.

Can I be fined for not paying the Poll Tax? No, there are no fines for not paying the Poll Tax. However, the question of fines can arise under the breach of the duty of a debtor to supply information requested by a local authority.

Can my bank account be arrested? There is no power to arrest bank accounts, this is possible in Scotland but not in England and Wales.

ATTACHMENT OF EARNINGS

Can my pension, student grant or income other than income support, wages or salary be subject to deductions? The legislation only provides for attachment of earnings or deductions from income support. It would therefore appear that any income which is not earnings or income support cannot be subject to attachment or deduction orders.

Attachment of Earnings

What is an attachment of earnings order? An attachment of earnings order is an order drawn up by the local authority and served on an employer. The employer must comply with the order and deduct Poll Tax from the wages of a debtor and pay it directly to the local authority. Attachment of earnings orders may be used for the recovery of fines or debts, they are not peculiar to Poll Tax. The Poll Tax legislation even provides for people who already have such an order on their wages.

What renders attachment of earnings orders ineffective? Attachment of earnings orders become ineffective if the debtor becomes self-employed, unemployed or changes work. In order to get around this, the Poll Tax legislation imposes duties on both employers and debtors.

What duties must an employer perform? An employer who employs a Poll Tax debtor subject to an attachment to earnings order must:
  i) Notify the debtor in writing each time a deduction is made.
  ii) Give notification to the debtor at the time the pay statement

ATTACHMENT OF EARNINGS

is given or, if no pay statement is given, as soon as is practicable.
iii) Notify the local authority within 14 days if the debtor leaves their employment. Or, within 14 days from when the employer knew of the debtors attachment of earnings order.

If the employer fails in these duties s/he may be liable for a criminal conviction and a fine. An employer risks a conviction and a fine not exceeding £100 for failing to comply with these duties and up to but not exceeding £400 if false information is given knowingly or recklessly. Understandably, many employers are not keen on becoming local authority debt collectors.

Can my employer make any additional deductions?

Where you become subject to an attachment of earnings order, your employer is entitled to take £1 to cover administrative costs for each occasion a deduction is made. For people paid daily the amounts deducted could become considerable.

What are the duties of a debtor?

A debtor who is subject to an attachment of earnings order is required to notify the local authority each time s/he leaves a job, starts a new one or returns to a previous employer.

The debtor is expected to tell the local authority:
i) "So far as he is able" the expected earnings from the employment concerned.
ii) The deductions or expected deductions (if the debtor can) from the earnings due to income tax and national insurance.
iii) The name and the address of the employer.
iv) Details of any work number or identity number at the work place.

The debtor is expected to provide this information within 14 days of either leaving, commencing or recommencing employment, as the case may be, or within 14 days from when the local authority informs the debtor that the attachment of earnings order has been made.

One problem that may arise is that it is sometimes difficult to precisely identify exactly when a debtor is actually in employment.

ATTACHMENT OF EARNINGS

This has been a problem in employment law in the past, particularly where an individual may be self-employed on occasions or is involved in complicated sub-contracting arrangements involving different employers.

What happens if a debtor fails to give information to the authority? A debtor who fails to give the required information risks a conviction and a fine not exceeding £100. This is one of the few aspects of Poll Tax legislation which involves the criminal law and involves the criminal jurisdiction of the Magistrates' Court.

If a debtor knowingly or recklessly gives false information on a relevant fact to a local authority the penalty could be even higher with a fine of up to £400. However, if a debtor makes a genuine mistake in the course of acting honestly or if the error lies with the way the local authority interpreted the information (given there should be a defence to any criminal proceedings) the likelihood of prosecution is probably small. However, the fact that the risk is there shows the importance of looking after all correspondence and making copies of anything you send to your local authority in the event of any problem arising.

What if I am subject to one or more attachment of earnings orders already? Where an employer is already required to deduct from your earnings under an existing attachment of earnings order, for example for a County Court judgement or an unpaid fine, the employer must only make deductions on the first order. When that has expired the attachment of earnings order from your local authority comes into force. The purpose of the government seems to be two fold – to stop anyone being overburdened with debt and also to make local authorities wait for their money. Where a Poll Tax attachment of earnings order is made first, any second order will be deducted from the remaining wages.

ATTACHMENT OF EARNINGS

What if I am employed as a civil servant? If you are a civil servant your employer is classed as being the chief officer of the department. Any transfer from one department, office or body to another is classed as a change of employment for the purposes of the regulations.

Earnings paid by the Crown or a Minister of the Crown or out of public revenue are treated as being paid by the chief officer concerned. Any problems that occur in determining who is the relevant officer or any other relevant matter will be referred to the Minister for the Civil Service.

How much can an authority take from my earnings? The local authority can only take certain amounts from your earnings. These amounts are related to how much you earn. It is one of the ironies of Poll Tax legislation that whilst the income of an individual is not taken into consideration when it comes to paying Community Charges, it is considered relevant if Poll Tax is not paid and an attachment of earnings order is imposed.

As a result, in some local authority areas with high Poll Taxes, individuals or low wage earners may actually be better off financially by not paying and being made subject to successive attachment of earnings orders. Given that a person can only be subject to one attachment of earnings order for Poll Tax recovery at a time, liability for 1991–92 Poll Tax could be pushed on much later into the decade, thus giving non-payers longer to spread their payments than those who pay correctly by the normal instalment scheme!

Deductions Under Attachment of Earnings Orders from Net Daily Earnings

Daily Earnings	Deduction
Not exceeding £5	Nil
£5–9	£0.20
£9–11	£0.50
£11–13	£1.00

ATTACHMENT OF EARNINGS

£13–15	£1.20
£15–17	£1.40
£17–19	£1.70
£19–21	£2.10
£21–23	£2.50
£23–25	£3.00
£25–27	£3.60
£27–30	£4.50
£30–33	£5.30
£33–36	£6.70
£36–39	£8.00
£39–42	£9.40
Exceeding £42	£9.40 for the first £42 plus 50% of remainder.

Deductions Under Attachment of Earnings Orders from Net Weekly Earnings

Weekly Earnings	Deduction
Not exceeding £35	Nil.
£35–£55	£1.
£55–£65	£2.
£65–£75	£3.
£75–£80	£4.
£80–£85	£5
£85–£90	£6.
£90–£95	£7.
£95–£100	£8.
£100–£110	£9.
£110–£120	£11.
£120–£130	£12.
£130–£140	£14.
£140–£150	£15.
£150–£160	£18.
£160–£170	£20.
£170–£180	£23.

ATTACHMENT OF EARNINGS

£180–£190	£25.
£190–£200	£28.
£200–£220	£35.
£220–£240	£42.
£240–£260	£50.
£260–£280	£59.
£280–£300	£68.
£300+	£68 for first £300 plus 50% of remainder.

Deductions Under Attachment of Earnings Orders from Net Monthly Earnings

Monthly Earnings	Deduction
Not exceeding £152	Nil.
£152–£220	£5.
£220–£260	£8.
£260–£280	£11.
£280–£300	£14.
£300–£320	£18.
£320–£340	£21.
£340–£360	£24.
£360–£380	£27.
£380–£400	£30.
£400–£440	£36.
£440–£480	£42.
£480–£520	£48.
£520–£560	£54.
£560–£600	£60.
£600–£640	£66.
£640–£680	£75.
£680–£720	£95.
£760–£800	£105.
£800–£900	£135.
£900–£1000	£170.
£1000–£1100	£207.

£1100–£1200	£252.
£1200–£1300	£297.
£1300+	£297 for first £1300 plus 50% of the remainder.

(SI 438 1990)

NOTE: All tables show net earnings, that is earnings after tax has been deducted.

Can I apply to my local authority to discharge an attachment of earnings order?

The local authority which imposes the attachment of earnings order has the power to revoke it at any time. While on the surface this may appear a generous measure which a local authority may exercise in favour of a debtor at any time, the real reason for this power is to allow a local authority to attempt another method of Poll Tax enforcement where a particular attachment of earnings order proves ineffective. The local authority also has to have the power to discharge an order when it becomes ineffective for any reason such as a debtor becoming unemployed or where the Poll Tax debt is paid.

Nonetheless both a debtor or an employer can apply to the local authority to discharge an attachment of earnings order at anytime. No procedure is currently laid down as to how such an application should be made, so a debtor or an employer should simply submit a written request to the Community Charge section of the local authority concerned. There is no right of appeal following a refusal to cancel an attachment of earnings order, but nor does there appear to be a limit on the number of times a debtor or an employer may apply to have the attachment of earnings order discharged.

Deductions from Income Support

If you are on income support and fall into Poll Tax arrears your local authority can, having followed the correct procedure, ensure that your Poll Tax is paid by having it deducted from your benefit before you receive it. This only applies to income support, and other benefits cannot have deductions taken in this way.

For the local authority this seems a guaranteed way of recovering money owed in Poll Tax. But in reality many local authorities suspect that the Department of Social Security will have difficulty in administering the deductions. Social Security offices do not enjoy reputations as examples of bureaucratic speed and efficiency.

In practice income support deductions will take a long time to recover the money. Local authorities will also have to consider the effects that deductions could have in pushing some families 'over the brink' with the reduction of benefits leading to family break-up and other resultant expenses such as providing accommodation for any children concerned, which will mean extra local authority expenditure.

The local authority, having secured a liability order from the Magistrates' Court, can apply to the Secretary of State, in practice the DSS, to ask for deductions to be made from your income support. Couples are jointly and severally liable. This means that if one partner goes into Poll Tax arrears then that debt will be deducted from your joint benefit. However, deductions can only be made in this way if both partners are named on the liability order and benefit is paid in respect of both partners.

DEDUCTIONS FROM INCOME SUPPORT

How much can local authorities take in this way? Deductions from income support may be used to cover all or part of your Poll Tax debt. The maximum that can be deducted is 5% of your benefit (your benefit divided by 20). A deduction can only be made if you are left with more than 10 pence income support after deductions.

Will it be equal to my Poll Tax debts? Not necessarily. Your debt may well exceed the amount the authority can lawfully deduct. As a result it could take local authorities a very long time to recover unpaid Poll Tax in some cases.

What if I have other debts being paid off through income support deductions? Paying the Poll Tax is not high on the priorities list. If you already have or become subject to other deductions from income support orders, these may well be given preference to the Poll Tax. Generally speaking the items given higher priorities will be essentials such as fuel (gas, electricity etc) and water bills.

As with attachment of earnings there seems to be the intention of enabling the debtor to survive to meet other liabilities and making local authorities wait for the money owed to them in Poll Tax.

Can I be subject to more than one deduction from income support order at a time? As with attachment of earnings, a debtor on income support can only be subject to deductions for one amount of unpaid Poll Tax at a time. As a result debtors on income support would have a longer period to discharge Poll Tax debts than those paying it, certainly for future years, if this is the only method attempted. Statutory deductions from income support could mean that Community Charge liability is never completely discharged.

If my Poll Tax is being paid through deductions can the authority levy distress? The authority cannot recover your Poll Tax by distress (see below) if you are subject to income support deductions.

What steps must be taken to deduct Poll Tax from my income support? The first step is for the local authority to obtain a liability order from a Magistrates' Court. If they get such an order the authority must then apply to the DSS. If an application is to be successful that application must state:

  i.   Your name and address, both names and addresses if you are a couple.
  ii. The name and place of the Court where the liability order was obtained.
  iii. The date on which the order was obtained.
  iv. How much the liability order says you owe.
  v.   How much the authorities wish to be deducted from your income support.

The order is assessed by an adjudication officer. This is to ensure that you receive enough income support for the order, that the deduction is not more than 5% of your income support, and to assess the priority of Poll Tax deduction as opposed to other deductions that might already be in force. The adjudicator should determine these questions within 14 days (although this is not compulsory).

Will I be told if deductions are to be made? Yes, the DSS will inform you in writing of a decision to deduct Poll Tax. You will also be told of your right to appeal.

Can I appeal? You can appeal on the basis of not receiving enough income support to allow the deduction, i.e. your deduction is greater than 5% of your income support and/or you have debts that might be of greater priority than Poll Tax.

When deductions are made from income support an adjudicator

DEDUCTIONS FROM INCOME SUPPORT

assesses an authority's liability order. The adjudicator makes decisions on whether other income support deductions (for water or fuel bills and so on) take priority over Poll Tax deductions and whether the authority's request to deduct income support is within its limitations. If a debtor is aggrieved by these decisions then they should appeal.

Initially you should appeal to your social security office. You must do this within 3 months of the date when notice of the adjudicator's decision was given. Use relevant forms if available (ask at your DSS office). And remember you must set out your grievances in written form. If you cannot get a form then write to your DSS office. You should give your grounds for appeal, your name and address and the address to which correspondence should be sent if different from your address.

Who do I go to next? If your social security office cannot solve your problem or satisfy your grievance you then apply to a tribunal: you will have to attend a tribunal hearing and make your case orally. You should not be daunted by this prospect, tribunals are fairly informal and are not there to prove innocence or guilt but to resolve difficulties, and it is not normal to have or need legal representation at such a hearing. Your social security office should supply you with a form for this or give you the correct address to send your application to. Remember to set down the details of your case in writing. You must appeal within 3 months of the date the adjudicator's decision was made, not from when you received notice of it.

What if I am not satisfied with the decision of the tribunal? You have further rights of appeal, firstly to a Social Security Commissioner and from there to the Court of Appeal. But you can *only* appeal to these bodies if the tribunal decision is believed to be wrong on a point of law. To appeal to a commissioner you must apply to the chair of the tribunal in the first instance.

Can an appeal be decided in my absence? Yes, if you fail to turn up the tribunal can still resolve the case. But if you give a good reason your hearing may be postponed. You should submit reasons for postponing the hearing in writing to the chair of the tribunal, as soon as you can. (S.I. 107 s5–11, Schedules 1 and 2).

Distress

Distress is an ancient remedy that involves the seizure of a debtor's goods and property in order that they can be sold off to pay a debt. The origins of distress go back to the early middle ages when private disputes were often settled by one person seizing and carrying off the property of another in retaliation for a real or supposed wrong – private justice at its crudest. By 1267 the situation had become so disorderly that the King called a primitive type of Parliament together at Marlborough and passed a law known as the Statute of Marlborough. This held that in future goods could not be seized at will but that the permission of a court had to be obtained. This law was the origin of the modern laws (mostly 19th century or earlier) concerning the seizure of goods.

The seizure of goods to pay off a debt is known as a distress and the person or body seizing the goods is said to "levy" distress against the goods or to "distrain" the goods of the debtor.

The famous judge Lord Denning once described distress as "an archaic remedy". He was right. The Law Commission in fact recommended its abolition in 1986. Much of the law surrounding distress is very old and it cannot be predicted for certain how a Court might interpret it today. The reasons for the uncertainty are three-fold. Firstly, most lawyers never have anything to do with distress as their efforts are concerned with obtaining a favourable verdict for their client in Court – not with what happens after the judgement. Secondly, the people who are likely to have their goods seized are among the least likely ever to be able to afford the cost of legally challenging anything to do with the distress. Thirdly, many cases are settled before the goods are actually seized. As a result many of the issues have never been examined by the Courts to determine exactly what the law means today.

Distress can be used to recover the cost of rent owed to a landlord, for unpaid rates or taxes, for outstanding debts, and the recovery of civil damages or unpaid fines.

Who seizes the goods? The process of physically seizing the goods is usually carried out by bailiffs. Once a Court order has been obtained to seize goods, bailiffs go to the residence of the debtor (or business premises if the debtor runs a business) to seize goods which may be found. These are then taken to be sold off at an auction to try and recover the money owed.

Most bailiffs are employed by private firms who are hired by the party seeking to recover the debt. Some local authorities may also employ their own bailiffs. As well as seizing goods they may also carry out evictions. The High Court also employs officers to recover debts and property and carry out evictions, although they are not involved in Poll Tax debts. Not surprisingly, bailiffs are expecting business to boom. At the same time they are going to extraordinary lengths to try and convince people that they are socially aware and not 'the heavy mob'.

To practise as a bailiff a person must have no criminal convictions and must have been granted a certificate by a County Court Judge. To obtain a certificate, a bailiff must have £10,000 in a bank acccount as insurance and must have a knowledge of the law concerning bailiffs.

In practice, however, it is thought that bailiffs often abuse their powers by playing on the ignorance of the people whose property they come to seize and claiming powers they do not possess. It is therefore crucial that there is wider understanding of bailiffs, what they can and cannot do and what legal steps you can take if they do not act according to the law.

When will a local authority apply for an order for distress?
As with all other remedies, it is at the discretion of the local authority as to whether they send in the bailiffs. Local authorities are likely to apply for a distress warrant where they think there is no other way of obtaining the money. Some local authorities may adopt a policy of not using bailiffs where the person is, for example, a single parent or disabled. However, it must be remembered that any such rules are merely policy decisions and the Council may change its mind and alter the rules, when new Councillors are elected for example.

How does a local authority obtain an order for distress?
A local authority obtains the right to seize goods by distress after obtaining a liability order from the Magistrates' Court. Your local authority may inform you after the hearing that they plan to use distress, but they are not obliged to tell you, and the decision can be obtained in your absence. It is more likely, however, that you will receive a letter from your local authority saying that they will be seeking to use distress unless you pay up before a certain date.

Can I sell my property before the bailiffs arrive?
You can sell or give away your property before the warrant for distress is issued. However, once the warrant has been issued a gift of property to friends or relatives becomes ineffective and the bailiffs can still seize the property – assuming they can find it. Only a sale to a person prior to notice of the distress will be effective. The risk is, of course, that if goods are sold or given away to friends, the buyer is then legally free to sell or dispose of them as they choose.

Can bailiffs break down the front door?
No, bailiffs are not allowed to gain entry by breaking down the outer door of a dwelling house.

Indeed, their powers of entry are rather like those traditionally

DISTRESS

associated with vampires – they have to be invited in or allowed in by an occupant of the property, or find an already open door or window.

Bailiffs are entitled to apply force by lifting a latch or turning a door handle to see if they can open a door, but they are not allowed to use force to break open a door which is locked or bolted against them. The origins of this rule of law go back to Semayne's Case (1603) which held that no power to break open an outer door of a dwelling house existed for what would be today's equivalent of a civil case. From this principle the familiar saying 'an Englishman's home is his castle' is derived. Semayne's Case seems to be based on an even earlier case in the reign of Edward II when someone who broke into an enclosure was held liable for trespass. Nor can bailiffs smash or force windows, although if a window is already partly open it can be raised higher to allow the bailiff room to climb in.

Once inside a bailiff can force open an inner door which is locked. Although how this affects houses with multiple flats inside cannot be accurately determined until a case arises.

There is not a limit on the number of times a bailiff may attempt to catch the occupiers unaware and obtain entry. If bailiffs fail to gain entry on one occasion they may return to attempt to levy distress on another occasion.

Rights of appeal lie to the Magistrates' Courts for irregular distress to collect Poll Tax.

What should I do if I think the bailiffs are coming?

Try to ensure that you have at least one other adult present with you when the bailiffs arrive. This could be anybody, a relative, neighbour, friend, lawyer or legal advisor, or a minister of religion. If you are certain of a time you could even invite representatives of the press or other media to be present. You are also entitled to take photographs or film of the bailiffs who call.

It is important to have somebody present to act as a witness in the event of a bailiff becoming violent or committing some other unlawful act. Make a note of anything the bailiffs say or any powers they claim. Make sure your witness is in earshot. If bailiffs carry out an unlawful act or do something of which you have grounds to complain, you will need evidence to back up your complaint. This is provided by the account of the witness who saw or experienced the particular events concerned.

Make a record as soon as possible, in writing, after the bailiffs have called, listing what occurred; date it and make a note of the time. If any matter concerning the distress becomes contentious you may be able to refer to such a note – but only if it was made within a few hours of the events concerned.

What goods are exempt from distress? Certain categories of goods cannot be seized by bailiffs depending on the kind of debt. Under the Poll Tax, the legislation states that goods protected by "any enactment" are exempt. This is normally interpreted as including clothes, bedding (including the bed) up to the value of £100 and tools of the debtor's tade or profession to the value of £150. In times past, this provision applied to manual tools, as it can do today with a carpenter's or electrician's toolbox, the object of the exemption being to ensure that the debtor could have some means of supporting dependents. Today there appears to be no reason why other goods and property should not be exempt – e.g. a calculator for an accountant, law books for a lawyer, a typewriter for a professional writer.

There are also certain other categories which are exempt from seizure. The two most important are:

(1) FIXTURES – goods which are fixed to the floor or attached to the fabric of the building are exempt from distress. Basically, only items that can be removed without damaging or altering the actual structure of the building class as "goods". For example, baths, built-in wardrobes, cupboards, certain built-in hobs or stoves, kilns, furnaces, cauldrons, windows, shutters, doors and built-in wall seating are all examples of items that could be immune from the clutches of a bailiff. Probably the best test to determine whether an item should be classed as a fixture is to consider whether the item is the kind of item you would take

away with you if you moved house or whether it would remain as part of the property for the use or benefit of a subsequent occupier.

(2) GOODS BELONGING TO OTHER PEOPLE – goods that belong to relatives (other than a husband or wife), friends or other people (whether individuals or companies) are exempt from distress. This is a very important exception as many important items in a family home may be rented, on hire purchase, on a conditional sale agreement, or loaned to the debtors. Bailiffs cannot lawfully take these items away from a house. If they do they can be held liable in law.

One problem that will emerge will be determining ownership if distress warrants are brought on a large scale. It is surprising that hire purchase companies have not taken up this issue as yet, as they will undoubtedly become involved if goods on HP are removed in error.

In addition, where households are shared, added problems will arise as the Poll Tax rests on individual liability. Where a number of adults share a household bailiffs could have considerable difficulties in determining if goods belong to the debtor, or which goods should be seized to cover a particular person's debt.

Goods belonging to children in the household are exempt from distress. Where a person over 18 is liable it is only their goods which can be seized lawfully. Toys, computer games, TVs and videos, all can be the property of under 18s and are exempt from distress. (In Scotland toys were specifically made exempt from distress along with many household goods – presumably to avoid upsetting scenes which the media could highlight in full).

What about goods where ownership is shared?

An important exception to the rule that goods belonging to another person are protected arises where goods are jointly owned. Where two people own an item and one of them is in debt, bailiffs can seize the goods for sale. The bailiffs take over the rights of the debtor with regard to the property. The best way to protect such goods is to transfer ownership completely to the joint owner who is not in debt, prior to the distress warrant being granted.

Might there be other exemptions? There may well be other exemptions, there are always doubts and uncertainties in interpreting the law, and this will be particularly so with Poll Tax legislation. As stated above goods protected by "any enactment" are to be classed as exempt from distress. This is a particularly broad wording of the law and may give rise to all kinds of complications and legal argument. The government may have inadvertently granted exemptions to many more categories of goods than it ever intended.

As the origins of distress are so old there may be a number of ancient statutes which contain provisions which could affect the categories of goods that can be lawfully seized today for Poll Tax non-payment.

Similarly, it is not absolutely clear whether the government have thus included those goods listed as exempt from seizure under the Civil Debtors (Scotland) Act 1987 by the use of the words "any enactment". The historic relationship (if any) between the Scottish process known as 'poinding' and that of distress would have to be examined carefully to determine the issue.

There are also a number of absurd and ridiculous situations that could be contemplated from the wording of the law. For example, Poll Tax legislation states that the goods of a debtor could be seized anywhere in England and Wales by bailiffs seeking to levy distress. Apart from the problem of how the bailiffs would actually find goods in different parts of the country or even in the next road, farcical situations could be imagined with debtors living on the borders of Scotland and England merely having to move their goods a few feet into Scotland in order to render them exempt from seizure.

Most bizarre of all is Chapter 15 of the Statute of Marlborough 1267 which forbids the seizure of goods which are on the highway, unless a special Court order has been obtained. This provision still appears to be valid law today and could suggest that you merely

DISTRESS

have to pile your goods up in the street to render them exempt from seizure! Whether a Court would share such an interpretation is impossible to predict but it is illustrative of the intractable legal arguments that obscure and arcane laws could generate.

What happens to goods seized? Goods seized may be left on the premises in what is known as a 'walking possession' agreement. The bailiff will probably attach a label to the goods which are identified as being of value and then enquire if you are prepared to enter into a walking possession agreement. With a walking possession agreement you will be asked to sign a form promising not to dispose of the goods concerned. The goods are classed as being under the control of the bailiff and cannot be removed or disposed of by you – although you can use them if this does not involve damage. Belongings may be left for a further period, to allow a debtor to pay the debt. If the debt remains unpaid at the end of the period the bailiff can remove the goods and sell them at public auction.

If you refuse to sign such an agreement, the bailiff may remove the property from the premises. In theory, however, there need be no time limit between the seizure and the sale – this was also the position under the rates.

How can the sale of goods be stopped? The sale of goods may be stopped by paying, or offering, the appropriate amount (including charges such as baliffs' fees) to the local authority (not necessarily by the debtor). The local authority must accept the amount and the sale must not take place. The goods then have to be made available for collection by the debtor. (S.I. 1989/438).

In such a case, you should provide written notice of payment in addition to the money or offer of money, keeping a copy of your letter as evidence. If the sale has gone ahead unlawfully you may then be able to claim against your local authority.

What authorisation must bailiffs carry? The Poll Tax enforcement regulations require bailiff to carry written authorisation from the local authority which must be produced if the debtor asks for it. The bailiff also has to give the debtor, or leave at the premises where distress is levied, a copy of the enforcement regulations and a memorandum setting out the total charges concerned. The debtor should also be given a copy of any "walking possession agreement" or "close possession" agreement (close possesion is the same as walking possesion, but a person remains on the premises in physical possession of the goods).

What if the bailiffs cause damage to my property? As the powers of bailiffs are little known, the risk is ever present that they may abuse their powers in the course of levying a distress. To a large extent they tend to get by on bluff and the fact that many people are alone when they call – hence the importance of having a witness present, where at all possible. However, bailiffs are expected to keep within the law, and they can be liable in both civil and criminal law if they do not. For example, if a bailiff damages belongings or part of the property, or if a bailiff strikes somebody, they can be held liable.

The regulations do not appear to preclude the use of the civil courts. If a bailiff damages property through negligence or carelessness, the bailiff could be sued through the County Court where the claim is up to £5000. This would be a civil claim and could be brought against the local authority, the bailiff's firm, if a private company of bailiffs are employed, or even the bailiff personally. For claims of £500 or below you may be able to use the arbitration procedure in the County Court – known colloquially as the 'small claims court'. The advantages of the small claims procedure is that proceedings are relatively informal and that there is little in the way of costs – neither side can claim the costs of legal representation. You are entitled to tell your story in your own words and a registrar – who acts as judge – makes a decision immediately.

In the case of a criminal offence such as criminal damage, where a bailiff deliberately or recklessly carries out an act of vandalism,

DISTRESS

the bailiff could face both a public (involving the police) and private prosecution, through the Magistrates' Court in its criminal capacity. Here it is the bailiff who will be charged with a criminal offence. And privately, for damages, in the County Court.

Can I arrest a bailiff? Yes, if a bailiff commits an arrestable offence, a citizen may arrest the bailiff concerned. Criminal damage is one such offence with a maximum penalty of ten years imprisonment. However, in practice a citizen's arrest is a risky thing to do. Although the wording of the regulations on distress for Poll Tax suggests that the distress itself may not be classed as unlawful, if the bailiff attacks somebody, they have a right to self-defence, providing only reasonable force is used. However, in the case of violence or a breach of the peace committed by the bailiff it is submitted that there may be no alternative but to arrest the bailiff and place the bailiff as soon as possible in the custody of the Police.

Are the police involved in distress? The police do not play any part in the process of distraining the goods of a debtor, although they may be present to prevent a breach of the peace. This could include a breach of the peace committed not just by the debtor but by a bailiff.

Can I appeal against a distress? A person aggrieved by the levy of distress (a person believing that the bailiffs have acted outside their powers) can appeal to a Magistrates' Court. This right is available not only to the debtor but also to anyone who may have had their goods seized by mistake, for example another member of the family or a lodger.

To lodge an appeal you have to contact a Magistrate, at your local Magistrates' Court, and after giving the details of your story, request that a summons be sent to the local authority to appear before a Magistrates' Court. If the Court decides that the distress was irregular it may order that the goods seized are released and can order compensation for any goods that have been wrongfully sold.

Is there any other action that could be taken against a bailiff?

Private firms of bailiffs have to hold certificates in order to practise where part of their work includes the recovery of unpaid rent. The Law of Distress Amendment Act 1895 provides that a bailiff can be summoned before a County Court Judge at any time to have the certificate cancelled or declared void. This procedure appears to be open to anybody who has evidence of unlawful or wrongful conduct by a bailiff. The Judge may order a hearing and decide if the certificate can be taken away.

Since local authorities are highly unlikely to employ bailiffs who have lost certificates the possibility of such proceedings may well deter professional bailiffs from any improper conduct or abuse of their powers and bring some of the more aberrant members of their profession under control.

What if bailiffs do not find any or sufficient goods?

If bailiffs cannot find any or sufficient goods to pay off the debt, they have to return to the local authority with the bad news.

Under the rating system not much effort was made to levy distress as it was felt that the the threat of imprisonment was a better means of compelling payment. This may be the attitude with the Poll Tax where the possibility of imprisonment is an option after the failure of bailiffs to recover any goods.

It is suggested that the bailiffs must make an effort to levy distress before the right of the authority to try to jail a debtor can arise. The regulations states that it must "appear to the authority that no (or insufficient) goods of the debtor can be found on which to levy the amount", this after they have "sought to levy an amount by distress". The wording seems to imply that the bailiffs must have made some effort. It would probably be no good if they just sat in their van or never turned up.

Imprisonment

> "I note that your constituent describes himself as joint secretary of "Hackney against the Poll Tax" and has declared his intention not to pay the community charge . . . . The Local Government Finance Bill envisages that a local authority would be able to take action through the Magistrates' Court against anyone who refused to pay the Community Charge . Such action could include direct deduction from salary or social security benefits, or distress and sale of the person's goods, with the ultimate sanction of imprisonment."

This is an extract from a letter from Christopher Chope, then a junior minister at the Department of the Environment to Brian Sedgemore MP, concerning the case of Len Lucas, on July 15th 1988. As stated in the letter, imprisonment is the ultimate sanction where Poll Tax remains unpaid. The threat of imprisonment we have found causes great concern, particularly among the elderly and vulnerable. However, whilst being described as the "ultimate sanction", a sentence of imprisonment can only be imposed in very specific circumstances.

Even if the circumstances exist where imprisonment might be employed, the Magistrates still have a discretion as to whether or not to impose a sentence, or to suspend a sentence.

Imprisonment was a possible measure under the old rating system. Around 4000 people have been jailed in the last ten years for rates default which works at about one person per local authority each year being jailed. Under the Poll Tax it is impossible as yet to predict what local authorities will do or how Magistrates will react. The ultimate decision is with the Magistrates and they may be influenced by all kinds of circumstances, not least political ones. With the Poll Tax the Magistrates' Courts will have to weigh up making examples of those who have not paid against creating martyrs.

When can a local authority apply for a person to be imprisoned?

There are a number of conditions that have to be fulfilled by a local authority before a person can be jailed. These are:

(1) A Community Charge Bill has not been paid in full or in part.
(2) A Reminder notice has been sent.
(3) A summons has been issued.
(4) A liability order has been drawn up for a distress.
(5) Distress has been levied but has found insufficient goods to cover the debt.

Only if all these steps have been taken does the local authority have the right to apply to the Magistrates for an order to send a person to jail. Note that local authorities only have the right to apply where they have tried to recover the money through distress. There can be no imprisonment where something has gone wrong with an attachment to earnings order or deductions from income support.

How does a local authority apply for an order?

The local authority has to apply for an order called a "warrant of commitment" to try to get a debtor sent to jail. To obtain a warrant of commitment, a local authority applies to a Magistrates' Court. The Magistrates' Court may then issue a summons to require the debtor concerned to appear before the Court. A debtor must attend the hearing otherwise a warrant for their arrest may be issued. Alternatively, if the person is not likely to attend the hearing, a warrant for their arrest to ensure their attendance at the hearing can be issued. The arrest can be carried out by anyone to whom it is directed including a police constable, but the arrest can only be made if the debtor is in England or Wales. The debtor receives a summons to ensure that a hearing can be made into the debtor's means – basically to find how much money the debtor has or can raise (remember the bailiffs have already recorded that they could not find sufficient goods to be seized to pay the bill).

What does the local authority have to prove? In order to obtain a warrant for commitment to prison, the local authority has to prove that the Poll Tax debt arose through "wilful refusal" or "culpable neglect". "Wilful refusal" covers deliberate non-payment. "Culpable neglect" probably covers particularly careless or negligent behaviour which you should have avoided and which has resulted in you not paying, or being unable to pay, your Poll Tax.

It is not yet certain just how courts might interpret these words. The word "wilfully" has been interpreted in various laws in different ways over the years – but the best view is that it involves a deliberate intention to do something (for example "wilfully obstruct a police officer" under s 51(3) of the Police Act 1964). It is suggested that to be found liable for wilful refusal you do not have to be against the Poll Tax – you could equally be liable of wilful default if you were an eccentric who believed you were helping the Council by not paying it because you believed they had too many other cases to deal with at the moment.

Culpable neglect will probably be hard to define. Each case will have to be looked at individually and could cause a lot of problems for the Courts. However, people who have been forced to make a choice between feeding their children or keeping a roof over their heads rather than paying the Poll Tax ought not to fall into the category. The local authority may find it hard to prove that the debtor has been blameworthy in such circumstances.

What does the Court have power to order? The ultimate decision lies with the court : "If (and only if)" the court thinks that the failure to pay the Poll Tax debt was through wilful refusal or culpable neglect it may if it thinks fit:

(a) issue a warrant of commitment against the debtor. The maximum term of imprisonment is 3 months, if part of the Poll Tax has been paid the term will be reduced proportionately.
(b) fix a term of imprisonment and postpone the issue of the warrant until such time and on such conditions (if any) as the court thinks just.

Thus it is the Court which ultimately decides even if wilful neglect or culpable neglect applies. So even if a person has deliberately refused to pay the Poll Tax a Magistrates' Court may not necessarily send him/her to prison.

Where conditions are set by the Court and these are breached, it is possible that the Court still may not issue the warrant for imprisonment until a further hearing has taken place. Under the old rating system a further hearing was deemed necessary where conditions had been breached and arguably the same law applies with the Poll Tax, although the regulations do not state this specifically.

Can the Court write off a Poll Tax debt?

Where there is a simple inability to pay, the Magistrates' Court may write off or reduce all or part of the Poll Tax debt. (S.I. No 438 1989).

The power to do this arises where the Court has enquired into a debtor's means and conduct and decided that the debtor does not deserve to be imprisoned. In cases involving rating this power has been held only to be available where the debtor is simply unable to pay. In practice this provision may form a way of reducing some of the injustice of the Poll Tax itself.

What if I pay the Poll Tax at this stage?

If the amount owed in debt to the local authority is paid or tendered to the local authority 'at the last moment', which might either be before the issue of a warrant of commitment or after, no further steps can be taken. The local authority must accept the money or tender and the debtor must be released. If a debtor is already in prison and the full sum is paid the debtor must be released. Where part of the money outstanding is paid the length of imprisonment must be reduced proportionally.

Poll Tax Appeals

As with the old rating system, the Communtiy Charge has its own appeal mechanism. The body which will deal with the vast majority of appeals is the Valuation and Community Charge Tribunal.

What can I appeal against? There a number of grounds for appeal. These are described in section 23 (2) of the Local Government Finance Act 1988 and are as follows:

i.   Being included on the Poll Tax register.
ii. Not being included on the register
iii. Any item on the register which relates to your Poll Tax bill.
iv. Being designated as, or failure to revoke designation as, a certification officer (a certification officer is a person responsible for informing CCROs of students' status).
v.   Any estimation, by an authority, of your amount of liability to Poll Tax. For example if the authority is unsure when you became liable to Poll Tax and estimates the bill.
vi. Being designated as, or failure to revoke designation as, a responsible person for purposes of registration.
vii. The imposition of a penalty relating to registration.
viii. The designation of a building as residential/business or as subject to Collective Poll Tax and failure to revoke such a designation.

How do I appeal? The first step in making an appeal is to serve a *written* notice on either your local authority or that authority's Community Charge Registration Officer (CCRO). You should serve a notice on your local authority if you are appealing against an estimated charge or the imposition of a penalty. You should serve a notice on a CCRO where your grievance relates to any of the above grounds other than one relating to an estimated charge or a penalty.

Your local authority should provide a form which sets out what the authority needs to know, and they will also provide information on the appeals system. If, however, for some reason you cannot obtain a form set out your grievance, detailing what you are appealing against and why and send it in letter form to the CCRO or the authority's Community Charge section.

What do I do after I have served a notice?

You may not have to go any further if your local authority or CCRO accepts and accommodates your grievance. But if the authority/CCRO replies that your grievance is not well founded, or the authority/CCRO takes steps to deal with your grievance but you are still aggrieved or you have heard nothing after 2 months of serving a notice you proceed with your appeal by approaching the Valuation and Community Charge Tribunal.

In approaching the Valuation and Community Charge Tribunal you must again appeal in writing; your local authority should provide a form for this (when you start an appeal you will be sent a guide to the procedures of the tribunal). You must state why you are appealing and why you disagree with the decision of the CCRO or the local authority. In addition state the date on which you served notice on the CCRO or authority and the date on which any reply was sent. *Note* you cannot successfully appeal to a tribunal without having first taken the matter up with either the CCRO or the authority.

You must appeal to a tribunal within two months of the CCRO's or the local authority's decision. Or within four months of serving a notice on the local authority or CCRO if no reply was received to your notice.

You will be given 21 days notice of the hearing. Both sides will be invited to make oral representations to the tribunal and ask

POLL TAX APPEALS

questions.

You still have to pay the Poll Tax whilst you appeal. If you are appealing due to multiple registration you will have to pay Poll Tax in the area which registered you first until the appeal is decided. However, if you are disputing fines for non-registration, fines are not payable until the appeal has been heard.

Must I go to a hearing if I appeal? With the tribunal you will be given a choice of appearing in person before the tribunal or having the case conducted using written representations.

If you opt for written representation both you and the authority or CCRO will be asked to submit statements outlining your respective cases. Both sides will be invited to comment on the case of the other side. You will, after your case has been considered, be notified in writing of the decision. (Section 24 LGFA 1988).

What can I do if I feel an injustice has been done in an appeal? A tribunal may revoke, change or set aside a decision, if a written application is received, but this will only occur on a number of grounds. These grounds are: an incorrect decision through a clerical error, no notice of a hearing was received by either party resulting in their non-attendance, new evidence has arisen or the interests of justice require a decision is changed or revoked.

Further appeal lies to the High Court but this only occurs if a point of law is in question.

How do tribunals work? Tribunals are intended to be informal bodies for settling grievances. The tribunal's task is to act as an arbitrator between, in this case, the various state institutions involved in the Poll Tax and those individuals who might be subject to it.

The tribunals normally consist of a panel of three persons. One of these will be the chair, a full-time position. An oral hearing is public, although the public can be excluded if a private hearing is requested; this could be at a debtor's request or if intimate personal or financial matters may be disclosed or if public security is a concern. The tribunal may also conduct a hearing with a panel of two; this is normally only possible if you agree to it. (There may be other people present at a hearing, these may include persons training to be tribunal members, a clerk to the tribunal and so on).

Tribunal hearings are more interested in establishing facts and ensuring that the correct decision, according to the law, is made. To this end hearings are more informal and less legally rigorous than Courts. It is intended that you do not require legal representation to appear before a tribunal, as a consequence of which legal aid is not available for tribunal hearings. You can be represented if you wish to be and the person representing you need not be legally qualified.

There will be different tribunals involved in the Poll Tax in addition to its own Valuation and Community Charge Tribunal; as you come into contact with them you will be given guidelines for that particular tribunal. Remember, tribunals are there to be used and they are supposed to be 'user friendly'.

Cornish Tin Mines and the Stannary Parliament

The possibility of an exemption from the Poll Tax, arising through share ownership in a Cornish tin mine and the Stannary Parliament of Cornwall, has received a degree of media publicity and much popular discussion.

The position claimed is that by virtue of a Royal Charter of 1508 the Stannary Parliament of Cornwall has a power of veto over all taxes levied by the government on tin miners, descendants of tin

CORNISH TIN MINES AND THE STANNARY PARLIAMENT

miners in perpetuity, owners of tin mines and workers in the tin industry.

The argument is that the government cannot legally require you to pay if you come under the jurisdiction of the Stannary Parliament and you can only be tried for non-payment through the Stannary Courts.

On this basis many applications for tin mine shares have been made in order to come within the jurisdiction of the Stannary Parliament. In our view, whilst having no wish to spoil the fun or deter ownership of tin mines, the exemption does not apply because:

1. The Poll Tax is not a tax imposed by central government but a way of raising local finance.

2. The Poll Tax is in essence a rate rather than a tax.

3. There is no modern evidence of any exemption from other UK taxes under this charter of which we are aware.

Green Print

We are independent publishers of books on green and environmental issues. Our list is expanding rapidly, and is widely available through bookshops.

Most of our titles are published as paperbacks at very competitive prices. They cover a very wide range of interests.

To receive our catalogue and join our free mailing list, please write to Green Print, 10 Malden Road, London NW5 3HR.